Sandy Hook's LOST HIGHLAND BEACH RESORT

Sandy Hook's LOST HIGHLAND BEACH RESORT

SUSAN SANDLASS GARDINER

Foreword by Rick Geffken

Published by The History Press
Charleston, SC
www.historypress.com

Front cover, top left: courtesy of the Frank Smith collection; *top right*: author's collection; *middle left*: author's collection; *middle right*: author's collection; *bottom*: author's collection.
Back cover, top: author's collection; *bottom*: author's collection; *inset*: courtesy of the Carolyn Mcmillan collection.

First published 2020

Manufactured in the United States

ISBN 9781467145541

Library of Congress Control Number: 2020931989

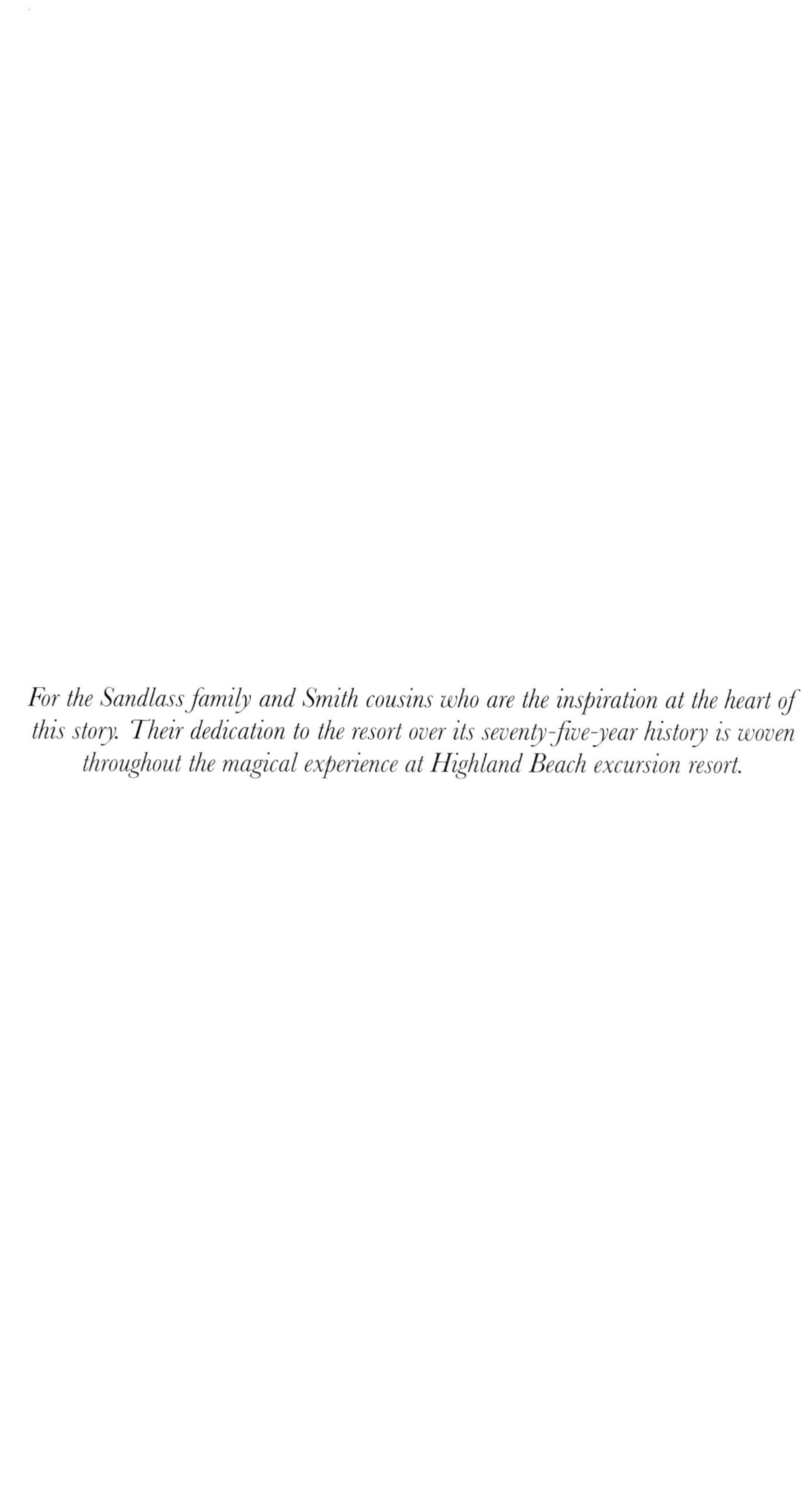

For the Sandlass family and Smith cousins who are the inspiration at the heart of this story. Their dedication to the resort over its seventy-five-year history is woven throughout the magical experience at Highland Beach excursion resort.

CONTENTS

Contents

Foreword

SANDLASS'S HIGHLAND BEACH

The earliest picture of myself at the Jersey Shore I have is a snapshot with my parents, Mary and Gip, at Sandlass Beach during the summer of 1946. It would take me seven decades from that moment to realize that we'd been part of the historic and important legacy that William Sandlass Jr. created at Sandy Hook.

My World War II military veteran parents (both army sergeants) had rented a bungalow from William's son Henry Sandlass for that long-ago summer. Mom and Dad spent many a weekend night at the Sandlass Bamboo Room club while my teenaged cousin Grace Ritzinger babysat for me. My father was a weekday truck driver then, so my mother and cousin took me to the oceanside beach almost every day—my introduction to sand in my toes and bathing suit, as well as to the cooling water of the Atlantic Ocean I've loved ever since. We were lucky middle-class folks, not unlike the hundreds of thousands who preceded us to this unique vacation spot.

William Sandlass opened the Highland Beach Excursion Resort in 1888, when he leased five acres from the Highland Beach Improvement Company, a company run by New York real estate speculator Ferdinand Fish. Fish wanted to sell land he owned along the Hook to rich New Yorkers and convinced Sandlass that a resort with rides, food and bathing would bring people from the sweltering cities down to the Shore. It worked better than either man could have imagined.

Fish sold his land plots, and his clients built their "summer cottages" (we'd call them mansions today) along the strip south of Highland Beach.

Sandlass became a wealthy man as he improved and expanded his increasingly popular resort for the next fifty years. Newspapers reported that over twenty thousand people visited Highland Beach on weekends by the turn of the twentieth century. Sandlass employed dozens of family members to work at Highland Beach for him, as did his son Henry, who took over after his father died in 1938. Henry and William's widow, née Helen Lynch, rechristened the place Sandlass Beach, the name virtually everyone at the north end of the Jersey Shore (always "the Shore," never "the Jersey Beach") recalls with delight today, though it's been fifty-nine years since it ceased operations.

Aside from the obvious amusement and utilitarian functions at Highland Beach in its heyday—river and ocean bathing, restaurants, merry-go-rounds, outdoor movies, starlight dancing to live bands, beer garden, music halls, photo studio, hotel, gardens and a pond—the place had a substantial impact on businesses in nearby Highlands and Sea Bright. Hotels, bars, rooming houses and breweries, as well as clammers and fishermen, in local towns all thrived as they accommodated the massive crowds visiting the area.

An immediate success in the late nineteenth century, Highland Beach also affected transportation infrastructure in New Jersey. Sandlass built a small steamship dock on the Shrewsbury River to make it easier for people to get directly to Highland Beach from north Jersey and New York. When the larger steamboat/railroad terminal at Horseshoe Cove on Sandy Hook was abandoned for a new dock in Atlantic Highlands, a railroad line was built from Atlantic Highlands to Highlands. A new "criss-cross" bridge went over the Shrewsbury in 1892. The Highland Beach train station was moved a bit farther south. From the south, a road from Long Branch was extended by the Highland Beach and Sea Bright Turnpike Company. In the early 1930s, New Jersey State Highway 36 snaked its way toward the "Million Dollar Bridge," a replacement for its cumbersome and dangerous criss-cross predecessor. Automobiles filled with anxious summertime revelers created traffic jams almost every summer weekend for decades.

For urban New Yorkers and north Jersey people like my family, the annual summer migrations introduced us to the prospect of a new way of living. When my parents, like so many former Depression-era children and World War II survivors, took my sister Nancy and me to Highlands during the summers between our grade-school years, they realized that living at the Shore could be better than in the crowded metropolitan exurbs. In 1963, we moved to Middletown, escaping the growing congestion of the cities and towns near New York City. I've no doubt that my parents' memories of Sandlass Beach and just-across-the-river Navesink Highlands influenced that move.

All of this because a son of German immigrants, William Sandlass Jr., had the vision to open his day trippers paradise to the emerging middle class in post–Industrial Revolution America. The man was an entrepreneurial genius—he put up the Great Switchback Rail Road, a prototype roller coaster a year after he opened Highland Beach. He built it, and they came—and kept coming. He printed thousands of penny postcards, which his happy customers mailed back to family and friends everywhere. It was the cheapest and best advertising of the day. A dedicated newspaper about the resort, the *Oracle,* touted its marvels.

When people's entertainment tastes changed, William Sandlass Jr. used the Great Switchback Rail Road's frameworks to build his family home on Highland Beach. They lived upstairs, above a bowling alley and a pool hall, a grocery store, then a tavern. When the federal government forced the Sandlass family to move the house so it could widen a road into Fort Hancock at the tip of the Hook, Henry Sandlass used its components for his own home and the Bamboo Room both closer to the river. The house still stands today, dilapidated, sure, but the last remnant of a once glorious place and time.

This book, written by William Sandlass Jr.'s granddaughter Susie, celebrates the grandest and, paradoxically, least remembered of the many "amusement parks" along the Shore. In it, she lovingly portrays the man Susie never knew—he died several years before she was born and raised in the home he built. Susie has kept alive the memory, the images, the artifacts and the family stories of Highland Beach throughout her life, even while she and husband Gary Gardiner raised their five children. She presents all of these to us in this carefully researched and rendered volume from The History Press. Susie's own vision (which includes her time as the driving force behind a nonprofit museum dedicated to Highland Beach) is why we'll always be able to recall and wonder at William Sandlass Jr.'s unique contribution to our shared heritage.

I couldn't be prouder to know her and to add my modest memories to this impressive work.

—Rick Geffken
Farmingdale NJ

ACKNOWLEDGEMENTS

The journey to tell this tale began in 2003, when I encountered National Park Service historian Tom Hoffman at Sandy Hook Park (Gateway National Recreation Area). His inquisitiveness about history and the Sandlass Pavilion House could not be denied. The conversation began that day, and we soon agreed to exchange information and share Sandlass family artifacts to unearth the story of the forgotten resort at Highland Beach, Sandy Hook. A family reunion at Bahrs revived our memories. We were face-to-face with the Sandlass House across the river. Cousin Frank "Blackie" Smith drove his father, Fran, to the gathering. The memories shared at lunch and a walk around the Sandlass property were all we needed to relive the magic we all experienced during those unforgettable summers. There was something exceptional about the place.

My thanks to cousin Frank for his discovery of more than five hundred articles about Highland Beach, enabling us to tell the story as it unfolded through the decades. Frank's dedication to weekly conference calls to provide Highland Beach memories and anecdotes to fill in the personal stories and his assistance reviewing text were essential since he was someone who spent summers at the resort. An exceptional documentary put together over nine months filled with stories of family remembrances is at the heart of the Highland Beach memories.

I am grateful to Chris Brenner for presenting an extraordinary view of the part played by Highland Beach in his family and in American history. Chris received overwhelming public acclaim for his film, *Destinations Past: Highland*

Beach, by the 2017 New Jersey Garden State Film Festival and lovers of the Jersey Shore. John King, a New Jersey historian and friend, first suggested a book in 2012 to preserve the lost history. My research started then and continued until this year, when I actively compiled a manuscript to tell the story. He encouraged me every step of the way. Research articles popped up on my computer to keep the discovery and curiosity alive. He succeeded! Rick Geffken, an avid historic preservationist and author, came forward to write articles and the Sandass House historic preservation applications.

The Bahrs family members, Becky and Jay Cosgrove, hosted us during many visits to their home as we pored over hundreds of historic photos linked to the resort and their Bahrs restaurant history. Sean Moran stepped forward to initiate interest in a nonprofit organization supporting the historic preservation effort to save the legacy of Highland Beach, an extraordinary excursion resort at the beginning of tourism on the Jersey Shore, and to tell the story of founder William Sandlass, a hotel and bathing beach pioneer.

Our Jersey Coast Heritage Museum nonprofit members supported us over three years to develop a Highland Beach historical exhibit at Twin Lights: Jeff Tyler, Jay Anderson, Felicia Campanella, Chris Brenner, Mark Aikins, Hank Sandlass, Lynn Fylak, Don Krueger, Barbara Krueger, Sharon Hazard, Courtney Cordaro, Frank Smith, Rick Geffken and Sean Moran.

I thank Dina Long, the former mayor of Sea Bright, New Jersey, for her encouraging support and her brainstorming as part of our goal to preserve the Sandlass House. An additional thanks to Mark Stewart, secretary/treasurer of the Twin Lights Historical Society, who endeavored to include the Highland Beach story in his "Day at the Beach" Twin Lights Museum exhibit. Thanks to all the local historical societies in the Bayshore area that have shared their photos, histories and stories during the last several years: Russ Card, Carla Cefalo, Walt and Linda Guenther, Greg Kelly, Joe Hammond and Sheila Weinstock.

My thanks go to New Jersey historian Randy Gabrielan, for contributing research materials, and Gary Sammon, for giving us access to the Rumson History Room Archives and Local Maps. A special thanks to Pete McCarthy, the unit coordinator at Sandy Hook, for his encouragement in seeking a future location for the 1893 Sandlass Pavilion House over the past few years.

Ranger Dennis Soyka hosted us as guests in the former Sandlass home that he and his family shared while working for the National Park Service at Sandy Hook, New Jersey. Margaret Westfield and her colleague, Sheila Koehler, architectural preservationists, provided research in identifying unique characteristics of the Highland Beach architecture. Jean Howson

Sandlass Pavilion House, the last remaining building from the Highland Beach excursion resort, at the southern end of Sandy Hook, New Jersey, 2015. *Author's collection.*

did an exceptional job in uncovering the transportation history of Highlands and Highland Beach. Thanks to John Schneider, for his historical videos of Sandy Hook.

My gratitude goes out to all my Sandlass family members (Ann, Duffy, Hank and Sheila) and friends who have shared their personal stories about summers at Sandlass Beach. My husband Gary and the support of our five children (Zand, Gary [Jr.], Kevin, Ted and Sean) and their spouses in making suggestions, doing reviews of my narrative and offering encouragement to tell the story. It made all the difference. Our grandchildren are always there to provide their love and ideas. Appreciation goes to all my cousins who have shared their touching experiences when passing through our lives at the beach as we grew up together. Unforgettable! Most importantly, appreciation for the patience of History Press editor Rick Delaney and the confidence of editor Banks Smither, who believe this is a story worth telling.

Introduction

LENAPE AND PRE-RESORT YEARS

This innocent strip of sand looks like many others on the Atlantic coast and if you've ever been out to Sandy Hook, New Jersey, you've passed right by here. You might not have realized that at one time, this spot was the home to a storied summer playground that provided years of memories for hundreds of thousands of visitors.
—*Chris Brenner,* Destinations Past: Highland Beach *documentary, 2017*

The barrier spit of Sandy Hook, New Jersey, is approximately six miles in length and forms a peninsula once inhabited by the Lenape and Delaware tribes. Their lives depended on the simple but abundant provisions of nature in the surrounding area, where the harmony of their existence was acknowledged when the first explorers sailed to this coastline. Giovanni da Verrazano's and Henry Hudson's age of exploration challenged the heritage of the early Native American inhabitants of Sandy Hook. The tribes encountered by the early explorers roamed freely over this larger area known today as the Garden State. Rather than being nomadic groups, New Jersey's Lenape tribe built permanent homesteads growing agricultural crops as a forerunner to New Jersey's current agricultural heritage. Hunting and fishing sustained the needs of the tribe on Sandy Hook, which harvested shellfish and seafood in addition to deer, elk and bear meat.

As early as 1524, Verrazano's ship sailed up the northeast coastline, being the first to sight the natives, as revealed in his report of the journey. In 1609, Henry Hudson sailed up the coast on behalf of the Dutch government. Hudson's voyage, seeking a northwest passage to China, turned into an

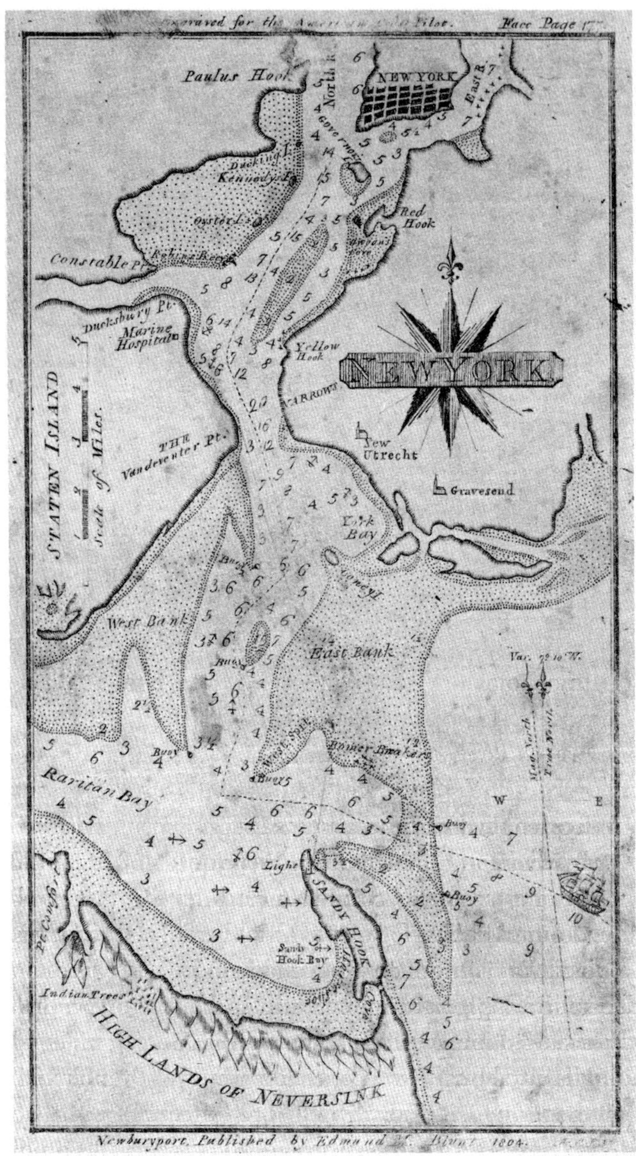

Edmund Blunt's chart of New York's Lower Bay via the natural channel at Sandy Hook's tip. *The American Coast Pilot*, 1804. *Courtesy of George H. Moss Jr. collection.*

expedition that encountered many tribes along the northeast coast. In September, his ship, the *Half Moon*, anchored in Sandy Hook Bay. At this time, the tribe on Sandy Hook called itself the Lenni Lenape. Robert Juet, an Englishman traveling with Hudson, detailed the historic first encounter when he described scenes of this peaceful tribal village on the peninsula and the Lenape reaction to the *Half Moon*. Juet noted that the natives witnessed a huge house floating toward them with people in it. On the first day, the natives boarded the ship to trade gifts. The sailors went on land the following day to explore the woods (Highlands of Navesink) and visit the Lenape tribe. Henry Hudson's visit gave way to the discovery of the river that now bears his name.

The small native population existed in a sustainable balance with the natural resources on the peninsula. White settlers arrived, changing the land and way of life in this quiet haven. This coexistence gave way to a change in the balance of nature. One of the colonists, Richard Hartshorne, an early resident of Middletown, wrote letters explaining the great resources used in trade with the local natives. A frightening incident one night almost threatened the loss of land Hartshorne had purchased earlier. Local natives unexpectedly appeared at his front door to claim the property as rightly owned by them in prior agreements. Hartshorne determined that he did in fact owe them for property in the Navesink Hills and all of Sandy Hook. These parcels of land were not included in the previous land grant by the Monmouth Patentees. Hartshorne negotiated this considerable portion of land, and he continued his ownership of the tract without any evidence of further skirmishes.

One popular Native American tale that first appeared in print in 1765 survived for over 125 years in local oral history passed down through the generations. Stories of shipwrecks evoke frightening fears of storms and lost lives. This folk tale of a seventeenth-century storm begins when a young, newly married couple on a Dutch vessel are shipwrecked near Sandy Hook. The young couple, Penelope Prince and her injured husband, John Kent, make it to shore, only to be attacked by unfriendly natives. Penelope, badly wounded, seeks shelter in the hollow of a tree after her husband is killed. Some days later, a native Lenape chief appears out of the wilderness and takes Penelope to safety while her wounds heal. As the story goes, she married an older man named Richard Stout in New Amsterdam (Manhattan). No one knows how she went from a Lenape captive to a New Amsterdam bride. Penelope and her husband moved back to the Bayshore area in proximity to Sandy Hook, where they raised at least ten children in Middletown. Penelope's relationship with the Lenape tribe helped the family thrive, and she lived to the age of 110 years. There are many cases of natives adopting captive people into their communities. Some captives chose to stay even when they could have left. Her Stout descendants are numerous and, more than 300 years later, trace their lineage back to her. It is surely not a coincidence that Penelope chose to return to the place where she had been saved all those years ago. The treacherous waters off the coast of New Jersey would produce many more such shipwrecks in the coming years.

In the mid-1700s, a century after land owned by Richard Hartshorne was first considered for purchase, the merchants of New York approached Robert and Isick Hartshorne. They chose one parcel of land noted as a four-acre tract for the purpose of erecting a beacon on Sandy Hook. In June 1764, these merchants achieved their goal of erecting the first lighthouse on the peninsula to safeguard goods and ships coming into New York Harbor. This Sandy Hook location also played an important role during the War for Independence. At the opening of the Revolution in March 1776, the New York Congress expected the arrival of the British fleet at any moment along the coast of Sandy Hook. The British arrived at New York City and used the lighthouse beacon to guide their transport and supply ships into the harbor. The congress resolved to make the lighthouse inoperable by sending out orders to destroy the beacon. When a military officer received the orders to dismantle the lighthouse, the Continental army officer removed eight copper lamps, three casks and part of a cask of oil. There was no evidence he destroyed the walls, thereby saving the first U.S. lighthouse from total destruction.[1] At the end of June 1778, British soldiers marched through New Jersey to the Battle of Monmouth in the New Jersey countryside, where the British led by General Charles Cornwallis met General George Washington's Continental army troops. During the night, with the campfires burning as a ruse, the British retreated from the Battle of Monmouth and headed to the Sandy Hook Peninsula on their way to New York. Washington was able to present the battle as a triumph. Along the way, a British general, Sir William Howe, built a temporary bridge, revealing something of the nature of this exposed spot along the ocean on his way to embark from "Sandy Hook

The Highland Beach excursion resort at Sandy Hook, 1891. *Courtesy of the Library of Congress.*

Island." Occasionally at Sandy Hook, fierce storms forced a breech in the peninsula. The resulting inlet turned into an island until the sands closed the breech. General Howe and thousands of British soldiers amassed at Sandy Hook and awaited transport to Manhattan. The first placement of the Sandy Hook lighthouse, five hundred feet from the northernmost point, is now a distance of four thousand feet in modern times. Sandy Hook Lighthouse stands as the oldest working lighthouse in America.

However, it is at the southern end of the Sandy Hook peninsula that we focus our story. A large tract of land, formerly the property of the Wardell family and known locally as Wardell's Beach, was prime oceanfront and riverside property. Highland Beach Association purchased the tract of land to create a new resort in the late 1800s. This land development along a short stretch of this picturesque beach became part of the early tourism boom on the northern Jersey Shore in the nineteenth century.

PART I

Resorts on the Upswing

1860–1888

Live in the sunshine, swim the sea, drink the wild air.

—Ralph Waldo Emerson

1

THE DAWN OF LEISURE TIME

William Sandlass's iconic Highland Beach excursion resort welcomed hundreds of thousands of visitors to a peninsula called Sandy Hook in New Jersey during the 1880s golden age. *Sandy Hook's Lost Highland Beach Resort* is an American story that tells a tale of the spirit that lay at the heart of Sandlass's search for a space he could call his own. One of the first tourist destinations on the Jersey Shore, Highland Beach was wiped away by time, technology and politics, as Chris Brenner reveals in his documentary, *Destinations Past: Highland Beach*.[2] Now, lost to time, the excursion resort is rediscovered in this story as part of an era awakened by the possibilities of more free time than ever before following the Industrial Revolution of the nineteenth century. This history shares equal parts of a unique location, an ambitious young man and a transitional time in the American experience. It was a time when the creation of thousands of new jobs brought prosperity to the middle class. For the thousands who spent summer days at the resort, the memories are indelible. With pennants flying above the turrets of Highland Beach, the Sandlass Pavilion opened to excursions in early summer of 1888, awaiting the packed trains and fully loaded steamboats emptying passengers at its doorstep on Sandy Hook.

A small spit of land first named by the Dutch, who called it "Sant Hoek," the Sandy Hook peninsula is a barrier island located at the northernmost end of the Jersey Shore. It encloses the southern entrance of Lower New York Bay surrounding Manhattan as the bay opens into the Atlantic Ocean. The uniqueness of this location, in the shadow of the highest promontory on the

Highland Beach letterhead by architect Charles H. Humphreys, 1887. *Through the Bay*, supplement. *Author's collection.*

Eastern Seaboard, Mount Mitchell, gives a true land's end feel to anyone who comes over the last hill and arrives at the ocean. The narrow stretch of sand and dunes, a few yards wide and a half mile long, sits just under the Twin lighthouses and across the river from Highlands at the extreme southern end of the Sandy Hook peninsula. The Highland Beach excursion resort's story is forever connected to Sandy Hook's long, rich history, which extends from the peaceful Lenape Native American tribe who fished these waters to its centuries of military significance in the defense of New York Harbor and the eventual influx of tourism.

Sandy Hook, originally known for its fishery and lighthouse built in 1764, enchanted the passersby on steamboats as the new century approached. The first steamboat and railroad on Sandy Hook were built to transport visitors to Long Branch and the hotels in Sea Bright and Monmouth Beach. This early transportation hub was vital to the future growth of Highland Beach. Jean Howson cites in her report about Highlands and Highland Beach's transportation history: "Rounding the peninsula was a challenge to navigation….When the river emptied into the bay and Sandy Hook was connected to the barrier beach, the river channel was shallow and boats ran aground at low tide. Ships under sail would wait for the tide and sweep through the inlet. Landing for some steamboats became hazardous. The volume and regularity of steamboat traffic would be directly tied to the development of resort hotels over the next few decades."[3] Eventually, tourism would transform the area as local entrepreneurs began to expand the infrastructure. Steamboat travel opened a new era for Highlands and the barrier beaches protecting it on the peninsula side. The most well-known steamboats serving the waters of the Shrewsbury River had familiar names to the local residents due to the frequency of seeing them on the waterways. These steamers were especially crucial to the success of the Highland Beach resort in its location on the barrier beach: the *Jessie Hoyt* (1861–88), the *Helen* (1862–88), the *Sea Bird* (1865–1927), the *Chancellor* (1869–89), the *Albertina* (1881–1925), the *Jersey Lily* (1887–94), the *Our Mary* (1887–94), the *Monmouth* (1887–91), the *Sandy Hook* (1887–91) and the *George B. Sandt* (1888–95). The *Red Bank Register* reported on December 14, 1887: "A fleet of fast steam launches will run between Highland Beach, Red Bank, Seabright, Pleasure Bay, the Atlantic Highlands and Sandy Hook. The old Highlands station of the New Jersey Southern railway is on the tract. The name has been changed to Highland Beach."[4]

The transformation of the New Jersey shore began in just a few locations, including Long Branch, that attracted small crowds around 1800. The railroad services began in earnest around the 1830s with fierce competition, creating business speculation that continued to expand. Resort growth had been building up on the Jersey Shore. By 1860, the Long Branch and Seashore Railroad built a pier at Spermaceti Cove on Sandy Hook to accept ferries from New York City traveling down the line to the popular resort at Long Branch. The seaside town had been drawing an influx of the well-heeled, as well as the lower classes, attracted by horse racing and gambling. The arrival of President Ulysses S. Grant in 1869 heightened its fashionable reputation.

The *Sea Bird* (1865–1927) was the most popular of the steamboats operated by the Merchant's Steamboat Company. *Courtesy of the Cosgrove/Bahrs collection.*

The *Albertina* steamer (1881–1925) was the sister ship of the *Sea Bird*. *Courtesy of the Cosgrove/Bahrs collection.*

The Monmouth steamer (1887–91) was one of the most well-known steamboats serving the waters of the Shrewsbury River. *Courtesy of the Cosgrove/Bahrs collection.*

In the 1870s, Grant declared Long Branch his summer capital, the first of seven presidents to spend time in the area. The growing popularity of Long Branch brought increasing interest to the more northern part of the Jersey Shore. As early as 1857, an article published in *Ballou's Illustrated* featured large crowds of men and women enjoying the surf, fishing and picnicking on the natural barrier beach at Sandy Hook. The train stopped at local destinations in the nearby towns of Sea Bright and Monmouth Beach and in other small neighborhoods along the way.[5]

Over time, Long Branch became one of the most celebrated resort towns in America. The two-mile-long beach attracted tourists from throughout the nation. This was a time when "sea bathing" only permitted wading, due to the heavy weight of the bathing costumes. Early entrepreneurs recognized the value of the therapeutic effect of a visit to the sea. For those who could afford these trips, it was a welcome change from the heat and stench of the cities. Boardinghouses and hotels rose up to house the ever-growing numbers who wanted to partake in a visit to the shore. The high bluffs at the edge of the water allowed for popular carriage rides, which showcased exceptionally large hotels made of wood. The popularity of the place encouraged improvement in transportation, transforming the town of Long Branch into a colony of mansions. The town grew over the next thirty years with the widespread belief that it was the most elegant resort on the Shore. The opening of the Monmouth Park racetrack in 1870 brought out President Grant to elevate its importance. By 1876, gambling was introduced, again heightening its opulent lifestyle. Four more presidents followed: Rutherford Hayes, Chester Arthur, William McKinley and James Garfield. In the wake of an assassination attempt on President Garfield, he was brought to the seaside town of Elberon near Long Branch with the fragile hope that it would help him to recover.

Long Branch was considered a destination for the elite as well as the middle and lower classes. The spirit of the place had room for every class of person, shown by the mixing of wealthy patrons in the fancy hotels compared to those guests with the smallest purses in cheaper lodging. The stagecoaches that brought people over the marshlands to Long Branch stopped along the way to drop off visitors at places such as the Pannaci Hotel in Sea Bright highlighting the elegance of the era. Even moonlight drives by beach carriage to Long Branch along the coast became a popular mode of transportation. An early form of transportation, carriages met passengers arriving on boats from New York. Though a day at the seaside ruled supreme, there were other pursuits for those guests wishing to spend

A Common Origin...Different Paths

Monmouth Beach and Sea Bright began as a single property but traveled different paths to develop distinctive characters, resulting in a history that is a study in contrasts. Both settlements stemmed from a seventeenth-century land grant to Eliakim Wardell. Wardell's Beach was a name prominent on colonial-era maps. Its nineteenth-century significance is reflected by its inclusion in Thomas Gordon's landmark 1834 *Gazetteer of New Jersey*.

Mifflin Paul, a railroad executive, purchased the northern part of Wardell's holdings in 1869 with partners Samuel B. Dodd and William W. Shippen....Paul and his partners, built hotels and summer homes near the bridge (a connection constructed by the partnership that connected Sea Bright to the Rumson neck peninsula). A town developed around the founders; growth in short time spread to the North and South Beach sections adjoining on either side. Sea Bright's early character had a high public profile.

Monmouth Beach developed a character of privacy and exclusivity. Residential, social and recreational life centered around the association's clubhouse or inn and a cluster of houses encircling the inn....Many houses, often large, elaborate and costly, were built on the ocean shore of both Sea Bright and Monmouth Beach.

A common origin, although traveled along different paths, have both boroughs sharing a beautiful, although fragile, adjacent place on part of America's most appealing landscape, the New Jersey shore.

—Randall Gabrielan, historian

time engaged in local sports. Fishing and gunning attracted interest for those who wanted more than sea bathing.

As interest grew, the railroad developers arrived. This increased the pace of progress up and down the coast. The explosive growth of resorts followed over the next thirty years with promises of a new way of life. In the beginning, a trip to enjoy a day or week at the beach was difficult even from the closest places. Long wagon rides over poor roads made the trek uncomfortable. Soon, the availability of stagecoaches increased the possibility of a more pleasant experience with additional steamboats from New York. Sun and surf were the main attractions, with few amusements at first. The guests who had not experienced nature and wildlife in their immediate surroundings were captivated by going into the woods and waterways to explore the beauty of nature.

Tourists were eager to make a trip to the seashore in the late 1880s, and passenger cars were added to the freight trains. Interest grew to the extent that the railroads offered "excursions." The middle class was growing in America, and the idea of a day trip to the shore was within their reach. The idea of time off for a vacation took hold with the masses. Newspapers and magazines jumped on the bandwagon to boost attendance on the trains. Advertising and marketing became more visible each year.

Fervor found in religious tent encampments eventually spread. As early as 1863, Highlands' Methodist house gatherings had become a common occurrence. Devotees could spend a week or ten days at a camp meeting with old friends while making new ones. In Monmouth County, the history of Ocean Grove and Asbury Park were closely intertwined because of a shared border on either side of Wesley Lake and a common bond through the Methodist Church. The Methodist Camp Meeting Association founded Ocean Grove in 1869. The Methodists had the intention of sharing a community with fellow believers. Ocean Grove rented out tents with a floor and a small kitchen that increased in number to seven hundred tents by 1879. Asbury Park's founder, James Bradley, purchased land in the fall of 1870 and named it after Bishop Asbury of the Methodist Church. Asbury Park grew rapidly and had nearly two hundred hotels as well as additional boardinghouses and private residences, bringing its population of visitors to thirty thousand in the summer of 1889. While other resorts sparkled with amusements, Ocean Grove fostered rigorous restrictions depending on the church denomination. The gates were closed at 10:00 p.m. every evening and all day Sunday. No alcohol, no smoking and no carriages were permitted on the beach, and bicycles were prohibited from the boardwalk. Dancing and card playing were not encouraged. Religious services and camp meetings were held almost continuously in the large auditorium every day. Asbury Park was impacted by sharing a joint railroad stop that was closed on Sundays. A short distance down the coast on Sandy Hook Bay, Atlantic Highlands joined in the popularity of camp meeting associations in other beach towns.

The Highlands of Navesink built its own identity. A type of lodging was available in the form of private clubs that drew tourists from New York City. Guests enjoyed the exclusivity of an environment that ensured visitors' comfort and convenience. As word spread of this new accommodation, it increased the desire to visit the Highlands of Navesink and its environs. The 1847 Neptune Club was the first club built in Highlands near the water's edge on the Shrewsbury River. It was exclusive to yachting members and friends. The club provided its visitors with comfortable arrangements, including overnight rooms, a chef to prepare meals and a room for parlor games. The sheltered dock steered members to its doors. Highlands' growing popularity was honored by a song dedicated to the Neptune Club with music written by the well-known composer of Welsh descent John Rogers Thomas. "Beautiful Highlands" was one of more than one hundred popular American songs composed by Thomas. His song echoed the nineteenth-century post-Romantic era surrounding the times:

Beautiful, Beautiful Highlands! Above the rolling sea,
To breathe the pure refreshing air, Gives joy and health to me!...

Beautiful, Beautiful Highlands! Upon the moonlit night,
I look from out thy leafy side, To watch the Highland light!
Fondly its beacon is shining, Like some fair rose in bloom;
To guide the sailor safely on, Amid the rising gloom![6]

Clubs were an important drawing card for visitors to Highlands who wanted an escape to be with friends of the same class. Within three years, the Jackson Club opened in 1866. After summering in hotels, the members initially purchased property from Peter F. Shenck just north of the present bridge and a few years later built its clubhouse on Shrewsbury Avenue. The Jackson Club eventually opened to the public in 1868 and remained until it was destroyed by fire in the twentieth century.

Highlands was situated in a natural location for fishing and became a draw for tourists to stay in its hotels close to the nearby beaches. These hotels by the water's edge drew large numbers of families and groups to experience a day, a week or a summer. The luxurious hotels offered a social life with music, theatrical entertainments and dancing. The famous shore dinners with seafood as the main attraction grew in popularity. Proximity to steamboat and rail lines offered the perfect escape. Local resort towns nearby were easy to access by local transport. Thompson's Atlantic

Pavilion, the Swift House and the Lewis House accommodated the influx of guests in ever-increasing numbers.

Between 1865 and 1871, a Highlands ferry was the only transportation available for visitors who wanted to go across to the nearby peninsula. It would take another year before the Navesink Bridge Company completed the first bridge connecting Highlands to Sandy Hook in 1872. Following a collision by a sloop, the bridge was deemed unsafe, and it closed for three years. The Navesink Bridge Company repaired and reopened the bridge in 1878 and renamed it the "walking bridge," as it was also used for pedestrians and horses. The bridge's romantic charm added to the experience of visiting the natural setting surrounding the river.

"The Highland Lights," an illustration from *Harper's Weekly*, August 18, 1883, showing the drawbridge. *Collections of the Twin Lights Historic Site.*

2

RUSH TO THE SHORE

Jersey Shore land development companies surged in a race to build seashore communities in the late 1880s. These towns advertised through various methods of marketing by distributing pamphlets and other publications that featured the real estate ventures available to potential property owners. Spring Lake entrepreneurs advertised Victorian cottages on tree-lined streets in the style of the times. Improvement companies also appeared with the backing of the railroad company and members of the land associations in Sea Girt and Spring Lake. They designed a town plan that would surround the Monmouth Hotel. It was elegant, with modern amenities, including elevators. When the enterprise opened in 1876, it offered cruises on the lake and a shuttle to and from the railroad station in horse-drawn omnibuses.

By 1880, real estate developers were looking for an opportunity along the seashore at the southern end of Sandy Hook. Ocean Avenue was built next to the rail line on the barrier island. Sandy Hook's southern portion, a narrow area just fifty yards wide between the river and the ocean, was directly across the Shrewsbury River from the village of Highlands. State senate president Anthony Reckless and his wife, of Red Bank, owned the majority of the land. The Long Branch and Sea Shore Railroad Company sold the area known as Wardell's beach on Sandy Hook to Anthony Reckless in August 1880. The following year, in February 1881, Mr. and Mrs. Reckless sold their 1.3-mile strip of land for $10,000 (equivalent to $241,527 in 2019), including seventy-four building lots on Sandy Hook, to the Highland Beach

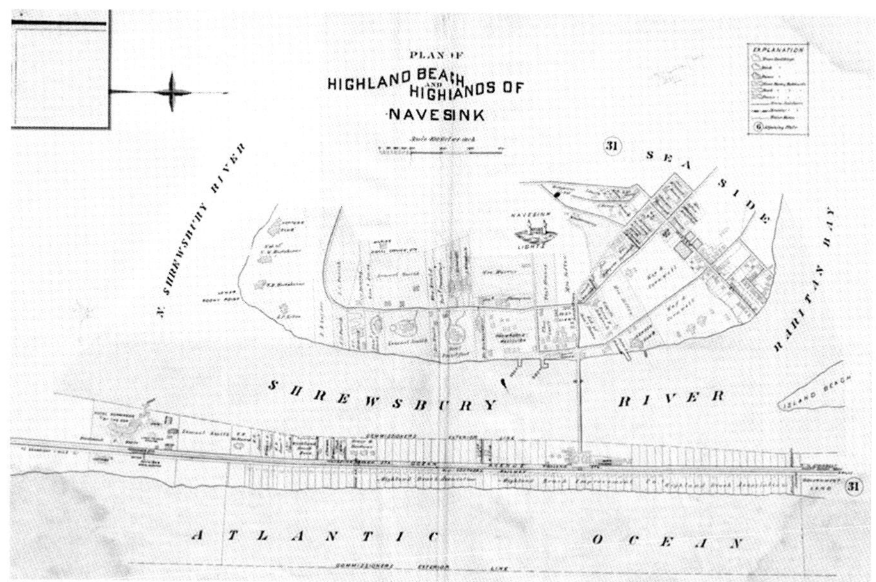

Plan of Highland Beach and Highlands of Navesink, New Jersey. *The Sanborn Map, 1880. Courtesy of the Princeton University Library Special Collections.*

Association. This subdivision of Wardell Beach was renamed Highland Beach. The Sandy Hook barrier island at Highland Beach situated close to Highlands offered the town across the river some protection from storms at sea. The small population at Sandy Hook included fishing villages and a few large houses used as seaside homes.

3

FERDINAND FISH, THE RISK-TAKER

In the late 1800s, the race to provide railroad connections to the Shore escalated. With the building of hotels, boardinghouses and seaside homes, a boom was created in the building industry to attract day trippers and more permanent residents from outside areas. The competition was strong among the railroad speculators over a period of decades as they came and went in a contentious business environment. The idea of beach access had grown to provide a place for all levels of society. The railroad men sold lots and built homes because real estate ventures were less risky financially than building railroads at the whims of external forces from nature and unreliable funding. The railroad companies produced popular Booster books. This form of advertising enticed buyers to their real estate locations served by the trainloads of visitors in the creation of "resorts." Free pamphlets were available to the riders on the train. Leafing through the pages, they could see what was available at each stop for opportunities to buy lots, with maps and advertisements and the benefits of each location. This marketing strategy attracted New York real estate developer Ferdinand Fish to the Sandy Hook beaches. The peninsula was within eyesight of New York City, an hour away by steamer. The desired arrival point was the northernmost location where a visitor to the shore could disembark and continue on to Sea Bright, Monmouth Beach and Long Branch by train.

Fish formed the Highland Beach Improvement Company and leased a number of lots from the Highland Beach Association to develop the land for an excursion resort and cottage colony at Sandy Hook. The new improvement company followed a familiar pattern that had been growing in seaside communities at the Shore in the late 1880s. As president of the Highland Beach Improvement Company, he started the building of summer homes promoted as "Cottages" or large seaside manors south of the proposed resort. He moved forward at the same time with steps to begin the Highland Beach excursion resort. The plans included construction of multiple buildings, a train station, pavilions, stores, a hotel and a restaurant. Fish's interests were strictly related to the development of the land, rather than managing a resort himself. He searched for an opportunity to find a proprietor who would run the excursion end of the business. He found that man in the most unusual of places when William Sandlass Jr. and the real estate developer's lives intersected in New York City at a most opportune time.

4

WILLIAM SANDLASS, THE VISIONARY

It had been just over a decade since cabinetmaker William Sandlass Sr. married his wife, Anna Elizabeth, when he came from Dorndorf, Germany, to New York City in 1853. Within a year, he sought a place where a cabinetmaker could feel a part of his community. He and his family jumped at the chance for a more prosperous life in a land filled with opportunity. They moved with their first son to the rural area of Shrewsbury in Pennsylvania Deutsch country. Born in March 1862, William Sandlass Jr. shared his boyhood with a large family of eight siblings in this rural town near York County. He lived at a time when the American Civil War came close to his doorstep. The Battle of Hanover took place on June 30, 1863, under the leadership of Major General J.E.B. Stuart's Confederate cavalry. As part of the Gettysburg Campaign, during the ride north on a march to York, Stuart's men seized over one thousand fresh horses from York County farmers. Once the war ended, the name *Shrewsbury* and the small-town atmosphere never left William Sandlass's life.

Seeking a life away from political strife, they found instead a society filled with prejudice against new immigrants. Eventually, his mother, Anna Elizabeth, wished for a more urban environment in a place with greater work opportunities for her husband and six sons. Within ten years, the growing family had headed to the city of Baltimore in the nurturing shadow of the Lutheran Church community nearby. Understanding the journey of William Sandlass's life requires a look into the world in which he lived. Will's parents struggled to speak a new language and adjust

William Sandlass and brother Charles in Shrewsbury, Pennsylvania, circa 1868. *Author's collection.*

to a new culture in America. While the parents assimilated into new communities, their children took on leadership roles within the family to assist them with integration into this new society. Their parents' adjustments to a new country placed responsibilities on the children's shoulders at a young age. These American-born children had language skills far beyond their parents, who were in the lengthy process of mastering a foreign language in this new country. The struggle to find a place in America they could call their own motivated the eight siblings to choose a path strongly influenced by the skills they had at hand. William and three of his brothers learned their father's trade of woodworking, which influenced and defined their existence as they adapted to the demands of survival and hopes for their future.

It is not a coincidence that some of the children in William's family shared the name of American presidents. A full embrace of this new culture resulted in new identities that aligned with the American experience for acceptance and pride of place. Even though the children were baptized with German names, they soon adopted the American translation of each one—for example, Ludwig (Louis), Carl (Charles) and Wilhelm (William).

In 1884, a Baltimore news article took note that the young William Sandlass Jr. and his new wife, Catherine Mattingly Sandlass, made a visit to Coney Island, New York, shortly after their marriage. Both William Sandlass Jr. and Ferdinand Fish had a similar vision brought about by their exposure to the financially successful resorts in the New York City region. The upper-class Brooklyn resorts of this era, Manhattan Beach and Brighton Beach, differed from their neighbor, Coney Island, known for entertaining the masses with its amusements. The two resorts farther east catered to a more elegant and cultivated group of people by creating lavish hotels for the elite and wealthy. The original real estate development plan for Highland Beach took root in plans to fashion the future resort after Manhattan Beach; "no Coney Island here" was prominently stated in advertisements.

William's plans were beginning to take shape when he and Catherine planned a move to New York City. He was a young man seeking a future when he moved from Baltimore, striking out as a champagne salesman coming in contact with every hotel and restaurant owner in Manhattan. The city in 1887 had a cosmopolitan attitude and tolerated many different cultures, a product of the diversity of immigrant groups. These immigrants settled in the city, and their numbers increased when the Irish population continued to suffer the effects of famine, which encouraged Irish emigration into the twentieth century. As a result of poverty and disease, an exodus to America took place. New arrivals often reunited with family members who had fled during the high point of the famine. In addition, German immigration was spurred as a result of the revolutions of 1848 in many European countries. In 1855, Little Germany had the third-largest German population outside of Berlin and Vienna when William's parents arrived. Germans were skilled laborers and craftsmen who settled in the neighborhood called Little Germany, or Dutchtown by contemporary non-Germans. This German immigrant neighborhood was located in the Lower East Side and East Village of Manhattan. The Irish families related to William through his second marriage, the Lynch and Smith immigrants, arrived during the mid-1880s migration into New York City. The Irish members of the family settled in the Kips Bay neighborhood on the east side of New York City bounded by East Thirty-Fourth Street in the area near Third Avenue to the west. Into this environment William arrived and sought his fortunes.

Playing cards and going to horse races were popular forms of entertainment during these early years in his life. At the age of twenty-five, his life was turned around when he and Ferdinand Fish crossed paths. The historian Rick Geffken stated in the *2017 Monmouth Roots Genealogy Newsletter*: "He [William Sandlass] knew the successful New York real estate developer Ferdinand Fish who leased some Jersey Shore land from the Highland Beach Improvement Company. To sell building lots for seaside cottages in what would become Sea Bright, Fish needed a way to attract potential buyers. Sandlass had just such an idea—put up a thrill ride."[7]

With William's Highland Beach lease from Ferdinand Fish in hand, Sandy Hook's excursion resort was born during this dawn of leisure time on the Jersey Shore.

5

BUILDINGS RISE AT HIGHLAND BEACH

Called Will by his family, William Sandlass arrived at Highland Beach with Catherine and a new son, along with a lease to build the resort in 1887. In the first year, Will Sandlass, the Highland Beach Improvement Company and president Ferdinand Fish had a plan for eleven buildings, including several pavilions. Construction of the resort started soon after the lease was signed. On December 14, 1887, the local press said that the Highland Beach Improvement Company advertised for fifty carpenters who would be well paid and asked for only skilled workers to contact the firm. The

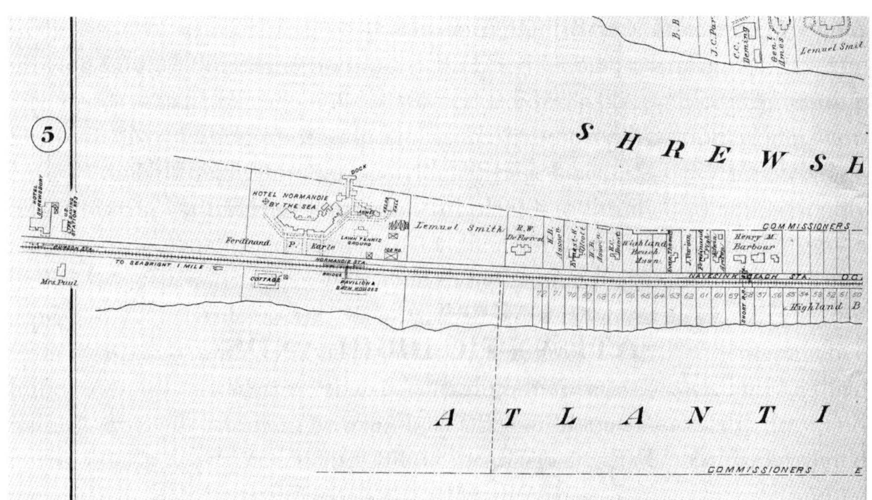

buildings started to rise on the oceanfront and riverside beaches opposite the little town of Highlands. Sheila Koehler, a Westfield Architects & Preservation consultant in Haddon Heights, New Jersey, noted that the Highland Beach resort architecture in Queen Anne style (pavilions, train station, stable, icehouse, boathouse, hotel, candy store and carousel building) was designed to be complementary and centered around the popular styles of the time: Queen Anne, Queen Anne Eastlake, Shingle style and early Tudor Revival, with some of the buildings combining elements of more than one style. She stated, "The expressions of the architectural styles are elaborate as part of the plan for attracting people by making the resort feel a little exotic."[8]

Will saw himself as an American who set out to reimagine a life in this country of opportunity. To say that he was the son of immigrants calls to mind a certain image that defined him. Being part of a large family that belonged to a culture that celebrated beer gardens and festivals, Will felt at home with the idea of a resort and included his German mother and American brother in building his dream, as earlier Americans had once achieved their dreams. The isolation and threatening storms soon proved a worthy challenge to their plans for the resort. The Great White Blizzard of March 11–14, 1888, was one of the most severe blizzards ever recorded in the United States.

Plan of Highland Beach and Highlands of Navesink, Plate 4, pavilions and summer "cottages" at Highland Beach on Sandy Hook, New Jersey. The Wolverton Atlas, *1889*. *Courtesy of George H. Moss Jr. collection.*

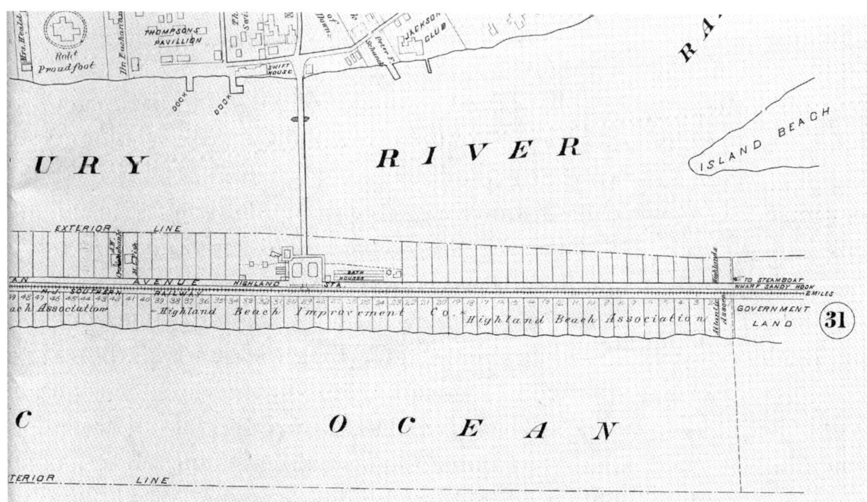

Life at the shore was a dangerous endeavor at times, when the sea roiled and spewed foam across the beaches. The 1888 storm took a toll on the construction of the new resort during the building process. The Great White Hurricane descended with all of its wrath when it struck on the evening of March 11 and furiously pounded the Northeast for two days. The sixty inches of snow descended on parts of the area. The East Coast was brought to its knees. The storm took the lives of four hundred and paralyzed the New Jersey coast as it moved from the Chesapeake to Maine. The workforce of builders struggled to finish work in time for the opening season.

Simultaneously, Ferdinand Fish developed the Cottage Colony for wealthy owners situated next to the anticipated resort. The two populations located next to each other would soon face the same challenges from weather-related crises. Everyone on the shore experienced loss, including this Highland Beach Improvement Company enterprise. The loss of life as a result of stranded residents and shipwrecks in the Atlantic Ocean was a high cost along the East Coast. Cottage owners

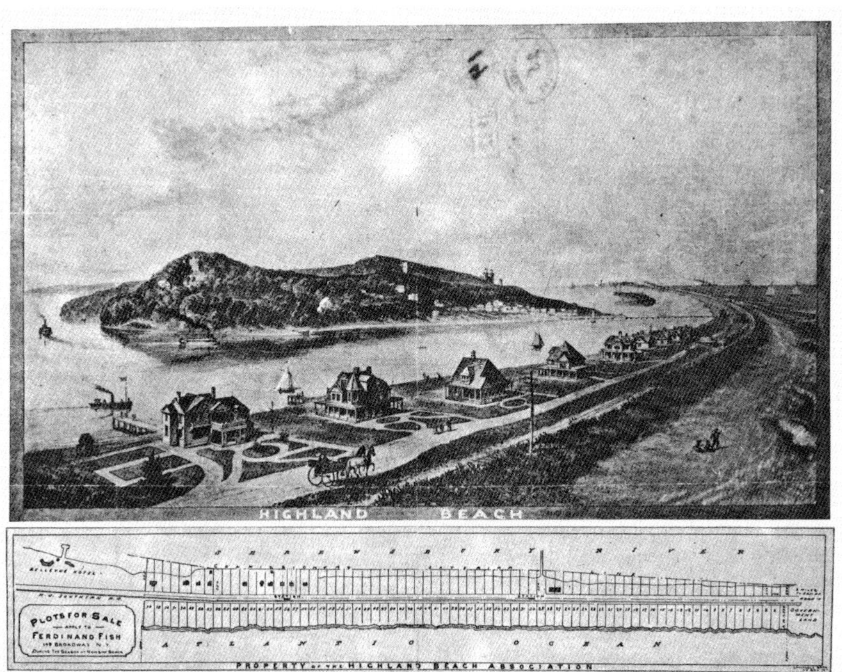

Navesink Beach and Highland Beach in an 1889 Highland Beach Improvement Company promotional brochure. Lots for sale by Ferdinand Fish. *National Archives.*

HIGHLAND BEACH

ON THE SANDY HOOK PENINSULA.

THE NEW EXCURSION RESORT.

A SELECT, QUIET AND DELIGHTFUL RESORT.
NO CROWDS. NO LIQUORS. NO NUISANCES.
UNEQUALLED SURF AND STILL BATHING AT ALL TIDES.
UNSURPASSED ROWING, SAILING AND CRABBING.
FINEST DRIVES, WALKS, GROVES AND HILLS.

Central Railroad of N. J., Pennsylvania Railroad, New York and Long Branch and N. J. Southern Railroad connections.

The section of the New Jersey coast nearest to New York has been made available to excursionists by the erection of a large restaurant building, a bathing pavilion, several hundred bath-houses, livery stable, boat-house, stores, swings, and other similar structures. The place is completely equipped with all the appurtenances of an excursion resort. Special attractions for small family parties or large excursions.

The Shrewsbury Dinner served to any number at from 50 cents to $1.00, by previous arrangements.

For excursions and dinner rates or other information apply to the Superintendent at the Beach, (Post Office Highlands, N. J.,) or at the New York office, 149 Broadway, or of railroad companies.

Here is what the New York *Star* says:

"Highland Beach is the first station after leaving Sandy Hook on the Jersey Southern branch of the New Jersey Central railroad. The journey down the beautiful bay was a fitting prelude to one of the most delightful days I ever spent. The beach here is quite narrow, not more than 300 yards wide, and lies about half a mile from the mainland, from which it is separated by an arm of the bay called the Shrewsbury river, which is crossed just at the station by a bridge. It lies just under the Navesink lights and the hills upon which these lights stand form a background of the deepest and most beautiful green, a positive pleasure to look upon. On the ocean side the view was equally charming, hundreds of yachts, steamers and sailing vessels constantly passing and repassing, lending variety to the scene. A first-class bathing pavilion has just been completed, which contains accommodation for hundreds of bathers. The whole beach has been graded up. Bathers have a choice of surf or still water bathing. An extensive and well stocked boat-house has been built and the natural facilities of the place in every way improved. The fishing is first-class. A seven-course fish dinner for the small charge of $1 cannot be equalled on the coast for three times the money, all the fish for which are caught within half a mile of the depot. Many new cottages are being built, and I predict for Highland Beach a brilliant future, which, if it does not attain, it certainly deserves."

A summer newspaper ad in the *Red Bank Register* on August 8, 1888, touting the new Highland Beach excursion resort on the Sandy Hook peninsula. *Courtesy of the* Red Bank Register *archive.*

on the barrier beach of Sandy Hook and residents in the nearby fishing village of Sea Bright were among the hardest hit by the eighty-five-mile-per-hour winds and sixty inches of snow. Will Sandlass and his building crew dug themselves out and continued work toward opening the resort as the summer approached. A major advertising campaign released by the Highland Beach Improvement Company preceded the long-awaited first day in hopes that the skillful and astute campaign would bring epic crowds to the shores of Highland Beach.

Advertisements in local newspapers both in New Jersey and New York City raved about the amenities being offered to guests. The resort posters attracted customers to the steamboat lines around the cities and towns. Rail lines boosted the new rail station at Highland Beach. The launch of this newest resort held the promise of opening the shores to visitors at the northernmost point of the Jersey Shore for the first time. Will Sandlass grew his dreams as Ferdinand Fish managed the booking office, awaiting the anticipated excursionists. With pennants flying above the turrets of the Sandlass Pavilion at Highland Beach, they waited for the first visitors to step off the packed trains and fully loaded steamboats. Highland Beach was open for business!

PART II

The Resort's Time Has Come

1888–1894

One of the first places to cater to the diversion-seeking masses was the Highland Beach Excursion Resort, operated by William Sandlass and his family. At its peak, more than 15,000 visitors a day used it as an escape from city life. The resort, which was reachable by train and steamboat, offered a family-friendly "middle ground" between the chaos of Coney Island and opulence of Atlantic City.

—Mark Stewart, Twin Lights Historical Society

Excursion landing at Highland Beach, New Jersey, circa 1894. *Courtesy of Walt Guenther collection.*

6

GOLDEN ERA ARRIVES

The picturesque nature of Highlands and its surroundings overlooking the Sandy Hook peninsula were described in the nineteenth century by novelists, poets and travel writers, including James Fenimore Cooper in *The Water-Witch* (1830), Walt Whitman in *The Fancies of Navesink* (1885) and Gustave Kobbe in *Travel Guide* (1889). These are among the more prominent examples that spread a romantic notion of the scenes encountered when visiting the natural setting illustrated in their publications. The points of interest brought to life in the authors' writings were close enough for a day trip. Views of the Highlands hills could be seen across the ocean from New York City. Historian John King states, "The New York City spire of old Christ Church was visible from Highland Beach but not the opposite—except that the Highlands hills were quite visible and also Twin Lights as well."[9] In 1826, the U.S. government bought a small parcel of land at the top of the hill above a waterfront tavern. The Twin lighthouses were built to provide navigational assistance to ships entering New York Harbor. They were instrumental in putting Highlands on the tourism map.

Along with the growing transportation options by steamboat or train to the widely promoted destinations, these accounts drew attention to the undeveloped land north of the popular resort at Long Branch. As the early-morning mists along the Shrewsbury River rose up to meet the summer days, the steamers *Sea Bird* (1866–1932) and *Albertina* (1882–1932) were making the trip past Highlands and the Sandy Hook peninsula and had been doing so years before the resort opened its doors. These early paddle-wheelers were a part of the steamboat history of the area that made it possible for thousands of passengers to arrive on the shores of Highland Beach. Built for the Merchants Steamboat Company, these boats were seen churning across the Navesink and Shrewsbury Rivers with paddles swirling in the waters and dark smoke filling the air as they headed down the rivers to the beaches. The railroad extended from Horseshoe Cove on Sandy Hook to Long Branch and towns in between, passing through the Normandie Station, Sea Bright (Rumson) Station and Monmouth Beach Station headed to its final destination at Long Branch.

The nearby town of Sea Bright had a simple beginning, started by fishermen who had built their huts near the shoreline. The 1800s era of growing resorts attracted more and more visitors looking for a place to rest, relax and enjoy the summer days away from the heat and city life. Sea Bright, Monmouth Beach and Long Branch were all inundated with tourists by the end of the nineteenth century. Residents sought a closeness to nature, pleasurable activities and ocean breezes along the Atlantic Coast. The freshly caught fish, fresh flowers and vegetables in residents' gardens must have seemed like paradise. The scent of the salt air and the sounds of chirping gulls and of waves crashing on the shore stimulated the senses of those living by the sea. The ever-present boats bobbing on the bay and holly forests within sight brought pleasure to those who sought nature at its fullest. Historian Sharon Hazard, in her *Dowager Diaries* about the Roosevelt family at the shore, recounts these experiences by local visitors. Sea Bright summer resident Kate Shippen Roosevelt and some of her peers kept diaries of life at the Shore. Letter-writing was a favorite pastime of the golden era.

Word spread as the possibility of a day at the beach beckoned. As news reports caused more interest in a summer stay at the northernmost point of the Shore, New York theater stars sought a summer getaway in an ideal spot just across the ocean from the island of Manhattan. Within an hour, they could be transported by steamboat or train to a cottage in the Hills of Navesink overlooking the Shrewsbury River bathed by cool sea breezes. Part of the major attraction in nearby Long Branch grew out of the desire to "people watch" when famous members of society joined the ranks at the Shore. Rides on the promenades along Ocean Avenue in a horse and carriage or walking the pier were typical ways to enjoy an afternoon of leisure at the beach. Carriage rides or stagecoach trips up and down the coast from Long Branch to Highlands played a prominent part in encouraging guests to spread their wings beyond the beach. A summer actors' colony sprouted in the neighborhood of Highlands just below Twin Lights, hosting well-known celebrities of their time. In 1894, the place had grown in popularity to such an extent that it boasted the actor Neil Burgess occupying a villa in the area. Historian John King mentions the constellation of stars residing in Highlands in an article about the colony:

> *In this summer actors' colony located below the Twin Lights in Highlands were such notables as Thomas Wallace Keene who starred in tragic roles including Othello, Richard III, and Hamlet with high acclaim for his "majestic method" and his handsome appearance; and John Webster and Nellie McHenry Webster who enjoyed success in both comedy and drama on extensive road tours of the U.S., Canada, Europe and Australia. Others in the theatrical landscape were John and Cornelia Wheelock, Horace McVicker, W.A. Hayden and J.S. Hoffman (later a borough councilman), all famous on the New York stage.*[10]

Ferdinand Fish and the Highland Beach Association sold the Highland Beach real estate lots to the famous and the privileged with wealth to spare. These lots were located within sight of the Twin lighthouses hovering over the peninsula on the opposite side of the river. Many of those who bought these lots were members of the association itself. The real estate development plan expanded the "Cottage" colony south of Highland Beach and built bulkheads with the hope of keeping away the sea. Emily T. DeForest made an early purchase of the land for $3,000. The Highland Beach Cottage development soon grew to include ten homes designed by famous architects of the day, including John H. Duncan, the architect of Grant's Tomb. One couple, Mr. and Mrs. L. Mortimer Thorn Jr., began their married life with great hopes for summer sojourns by the sea. L. Mortimer Thorn Jr. was the son of Leonard Mortimer Thorn, a millionaire from New York City who made his fortune from real estate and a partnership in a cotton goods firm. As in many communities, the names at his son's wedding matched many of those of the homeowners at the seaside Cottages and nearby locations on Sandy Hook at Fort Hancock. The wedding attendant and maid of honor, the granddaughter of General Winfield Scott Hancock, held the bride's orange blossoms as she said her vows. Among the gifts, an unusual dressing case once owned by Empress Josephine, surely accompanied them on their honeymoon to Europe. The couple spent six years at their summer Cottage before life changed in 1894, when their five-year-old daughter, Marcia, passed away during a summer visit. She was interred at All Saints Memorial Church Cemetery in Navesink, New Jersey. Mortimer's wife, Lily, daughter of

A girl in a horse cart with the Highland Beach Corner Store/Pavilion in the background, circa 1894. *Courtesy of the Isaac and Henry Vantine family collection.*

Nicholas Gwynn of the Cotton Exchange, joined a New York theater group in 1899, a few years after the loss of their child and the couple's separation from each other. One year later, Lily died without an acknowledgement of the reason for her death. The bittersweet nature of life follows the stories of the families who inhabited the world of Highland Beach.

By the late 1880s, the middle-class members of society could afford a trip from Philadelphia or New York to the beaches within their reach. Tourist guidebooks began to proliferate as members of the middle class became aware of the growing popularity of vacation destinations. Travel writer Gustav Kobbé found the Hills of Navesink in Highlands and Highland Beach a charming and desirable location for all those seeking to leave their worries behind while they rested and enjoyed themselves in the green hills with access to the open-air beaches. In the 1889 New Jersey Coast and Pines guidebook, Kobbé wrote about the new Highland Beach excursion resort: "Highland Beach is an excursion resort, especially designed for family parties, though larger excursions can obtain ample accommodations on notice. The bathing is especially fine and varied, the ocean and the river being but 50 yards apart."[11]

7

STORMS WREAK HAVOC

The perilous nature of raging seas posed a threat to the success of the resort. It was one of the first major obstacles facing Highland Beach Improvement Company and Will Sandlass. Following the extensive damage done to the Sandy Hook rail station in March 1888, it was rebuilt and positioned in front of the resort with the new name of Highland Beach Station. After the site survived the storm, the following months of September and December brought an onslaught from the sea that caused damage to the newly erected pavilions, dyke and other structures at Highland Beach. A drawing in *Frank Leslie's Illustrated Newspaper* of December 8, 1888, showed the "Guests Only" sign floating away: "The Recent Terrible Storm on the New Jersey Coast.—Scene near the Highland Station, on the New Jersey Southern Railroad—Gigantic waves sweeping across the peninsula."[12]

While Highland Beach flourished with all its success, it remained vulnerable to the whims of the weather. The ideal summer weather changed when occasional ferocious storms appeared in the colder seasons at the shore. Storms battered the coastline during hurricanes, blizzards and nor'easters. The barrier beaches that make up most of the coastline on the Jersey Shore are subject to varieties of weather influences along the shoreline. Most people wished they would never have to face another hurricane or blizzard, only to see these storms resurge time and again. The first year of business at Highland Beach was an intensely personal experience with the forces of nature. The fury of the sea was at its doorstep. The sense of destruction could only be imagined until the day when the winds ceased and the sun

"The Terrible Storm on the New Jersey Coast—Scene Near Highland Station, on the New Jersey Southern Railroad,—Gigantic Waves Sweeping the Peninsula." *Frank Leslie's Illustrated Newspaper*, December 8, 1888. *New Jersey State Museum collection.*

came out. Sandy Hook had significant damage, as the *Keyport Enterprise* reported in September 1889: "All the buildings at Highland Beach were more or less damaged."[13]

Another dreaded storm swept in from the sea in March 1889, when the "Mudhen Hurricane" moved up the coast from Atlantic City. On March 18, the *Passaic (NJ) Daily News* reported on the storm effects: "At Highland Beach the track of the New Jersey southern division of the Central railroad was torn up for nearly a mile. Heavy stones from sea walls were swept upon the station platform. Three feet of sand covers the tracks for half a mile."[14]

The precariously thin strip of land that makes up Sandy Hook has always been prone to the ravages of successive storms. Many times, the

Scene of train tracks being repaired after the "Mudhen" Hurricane of 1889 on Sandy Hook. *Courtesy of the George H. Moss Jr. collection.*

peninsula was cut through with new inlets carved between the ocean and the Shrewsbury. These breeches often close naturally when the next storm fills in the open area with more sand as the waves and currents move around the peninsula. A storm in 1889 destroyed two miles of track, requiring the railroad to build a trestle over a narrow stretch of the beach spanning an inlet created by the unrelenting weather. The New Jersey Southern Railroad (NJSR) had to wait until October 1889 to run trains across the inlet created by the storm. Hundreds of beachgoers routinely arrived at Highland Beach in this fashion for the next three years.

Due to the fears of future storms, the NJSR created a seawall that protected against breeches of the barrier beach between Sandy Hook and the mainland. These seawalls were reconstructed to protect the rail lines next to the ocean beach and the buildings on Ocean Avenue. It was reported that local cottagers left four to six weeks earlier than usual and cut the anticipated season short in the second year of Highland Beach operation.

8

PRIME ATTRACTIONS

Will Sandlass saw an opportunity to transform his life, and he seized it. The Sandlass Pavilion on Surf Avenue at Highland Beach saw dramatic business growth. The expansion of buildings at the resort encouraged larger attendance, with new attractions providing a kaleidoscope of amusements. A Red Bank owner installed a merry-go-round when he leased the space in the domed structure across from the Bathing Pavilion. A merry-go-round ride in nearby Red Bank cost five cents. The earliest rides had a hand-driven grinder who cranked the organ until tiring of the job. On occasion, the local constable stopped the ride and prevented some games from running at the Sandlass Pavilion on Sundays. Only sacred music was allowed to be played on Sundays at the resort due to local laws popularized by local Methodist camps in nearby Highlands and Atlantic Highlands. The Surf House bands brought in from New York City would be allowed to play only on days other than Sunday. All hands on deck required unusual living arrangements for the staff at the Sandlass Pavilion. The merry-go-round engineer lived in the Carousel Tower and the lifeguard, Harry Meares, lived in the Bathing Pavilion Cupola on the second floor. In the month of July 1888, the Atlantic Division of the American Canoeing Association was camping at Highland Beach while excursion parties were booked on a regular basis all throughout the summer.

The roller coaster seen by Will and his wife, Catherine, on an earlier trip to Coney Island was completed at Highland Beach in July 1889 next to the seawall by the ocean. The first and only excursion resort on Sandy Hook drew crowds each day by the thousands seeking refuge from the sweltering heat surrounding New Jersey and New York City. A day at the seashore promised bathers an unforgettable experience below the Twin lighthouses of the Highlands. Roller coasters had been thrilling spectators and riders nearby since the appearance of the gravity railroad in 1884 at Coney Island. It wasn't long before Highland Beach advertised a "Great Switchback" gravity railroad on the shores of Sandy Hook. The shout "climb aboard!" resonated above the ocean waves. Signs posted nearby advertised "pay a nickel and buy your ticket to ride the Great Switchback." With only gravity to provide the force, the early-style coaster hurtled passengers up and down an undulating track approximately six hundred feet long at a reckless speed of six miles per hour on the old gravity railroad designed by LaMarcus Thompson. When reaching the farthest point on a fifty-foot-high platform, passengers exited to await the cars that would return them to the starting point. Coasters were used to provide thrill rides even as far back as the first coasters designed in seventeenth-century Russia carved out of ice. Thompson had fifty roller-coaster patents recorded over his lifetime. Soon, his quickly evolving technology brought a new scenic railway to Atlantic City. The Great Switchback Railroad at Highland Beach became an issue

The Great Switchback Railroad (roller coaster) at Highland Beach in 1889, advertised as "The Finest Sport on Earth." *Author's collection.*

when LaMarcus Thompson brought a court action suit to have it removed due to a patent infringement. Thompson won his suit, and the roller coaster at Highland Beach was replaced with a new set of amusements to please the ever-growing crowds.

Business continued to boom when the Surf House hotel was leased to John T. Hayward in 1889 for $200 by Will Sandlass, the proprietor at Sandlass Pavilion. The Surf House and Basket Pavilion were the center for shoe-box lunch crowds arriving in excursion parties that included up to 1,500 people each. As visitors disembarked at the resort, the Basket Pavilion offered a restaurant that seated 300 with a serving capacity of 1,000 guests a day. The local seafood was a main attraction, and fresh produce was grown nearby on the grounds. Will's brother Johnson started a garden next to the Pavilion when he noticed that a lone tomato seed had grown in a pile of ash. He planted a variety of seeds to see if they would grow as an experiment. Soon enough, the newspapers reported his success as a main attraction at the restaurant. The menu held more temptations, featuring steak, freshly baked breads and confections. A full-service bar had been added in the open-air location with a view of the river to the west and the ocean to the east. A specialty, Mrs. Sandlass' Shrewsbury Dinner, was advertised on the *Sea Bird* steamer's voyage across the ocean heading to the Pavilion. A full selection consisted of steamers, fresh fish, seafood salad and desserts, all for the moderate price of one dollar.

This was the same year that a new steamboat landing was built in Atlantic Highlands. The Horseshoe Cove landing on Sandy Hook was abandoned, and a dock at Highland Beach became the first stop for travelers on the peninsula. Boating parties were prevalent in the waters facing the resort's river beach. One of the yacht's passengers heading home in the moonlight reported the fearful effect of sighting a sea serpent in the waters nearby. News reports appeared for days, increasing speculation about the effects of pies ingested by the passengers.

Guesthouses and hotels nearby and across the river provided lodging for guests who wanted to stay longer than a day trip. The closest hotel with a capacity for three hundred guests was Normandie by the Sea at the far end of the Highland Beach Cottage Colony. Despite the weather setbacks, Will Sandlass, his family and crew continued to grow the resort business. By the 1890s, they had added a photo studio, horse stables and pagodas. The *Oracle*, a resort newsletter, advertised a popular feature that recorded memories of the day: "Henry Vantine, the expert photographer, has re-opened the gallery, and is ready to catch the drops from your bathing suit."[15] Ferdinand Fish sat in his Highland Beach Improvement Company office connected by his new telephone, a modern tool that would allow excursion parties with thousands of visitors to book reservations with the touch of a hand.

Local news featured the approved business leases at Highland Beach as the resort continued to expand services and offer new amenities. Will was sharing duties with other members of the resort staff he brought on board to cover the increase in excursion parties and tourists. By 1894, the Highland Beach Improvement Company leased the Surf House and amusement buildings to William Sandlass and other operators for $1,100. Will Sandlass turned around and leased Conrad Stein the Surf House hotel for $1,500. It served as a center for hosting the excursion parties arriving on trains in-season.

9

TRANSPORTATION GROWS

An increase in transportation choices became the important catalyst for the development and growth of destinations on the New Jersey shore, none more than the new Highland Beach excursion resort. Ads placed in numerous newspapers in 1888 announced to excursionists the availability of this "section of the New Jersey coast nearest to New York." Families could leave from lower Manhattan in the morning, travel by steamer or a combination of steamer and rail and return that evening. A testimonial quote in the same ad from the *New York Star* described how "the journey down the beautiful bay was a fitting prelude to one of the most delightful days I ever spent."[16] The steamer would land at Horseshoe Cove on Sandy Hook, and passengers would transfer to the New Jersey Southern rail line that traveled along the barrier beach to Highland Beach, the first stop on the line that ran from Sandy Hook to Long Branch. Passengers from surrounding towns in New Jersey could use the same rail line from Long Branch to Highland Beach. In addition, the steamers *Jersey Lily*, *Our Mary* and *Leon Abbett* became regular sights along the Navesink and Shrewsbury Rivers from Oceanport and Red Bank, respectively, and would bring hundreds of daily visitors to the new Highland Beach resort.

At first, travelers coming to Highland Beach for the day would land on the opposite side of the river in Highlands and walk across the quaint drawbridge between Highlands and Highland Beach on the peninsula. Will Sandlass eventually built a steamer dock at Highland Beach to make the trip even easier. In 1888, a new steamer, the *Monmouth*, made the run

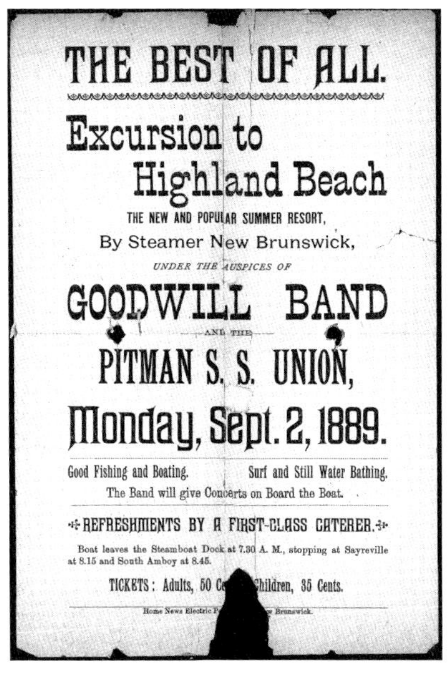

"Let the Good Times Roll! The Best of All is found in an excursion to Highland Beach!" Broadside Steamer poster, Goodwill Bank, 1889. *Author's collection.*

from New York to Horseshoe Cove on Sandy Hook. The trip was done in one hour and accommodated those travelers who had reserved seats on the train's parlor cars, offering additional reserved seats on the steamer, letting passengers avoid taking their chances at the dock. The rail line from Sandy Hook was improved in 1888, including double rails along the entire shoreline.

Expansion of the resort and an increased number of visitors strained their capacity. A well-orchestrated advertising campaign in conjunction with the steamboat companies successfully promoted the excursion resort as a destination between New York City and the Jersey Shore. The fast steam rides arrived at the resort destination, where tourists found hammocks, lawn tennis, croquet, quoits (ring toss), rifle shooting, archery, scups (porgies) and see-saws for a trifling cost. Touting features in the resort's *Oracle* newsletter such as "excellent drainage resulting in no mosquitos or malaria" attracted visitors to the beach. The promotional campaign was so successful that more amenities were offered. The business office added rented swimsuits, swim platforms, a lily pond, an icehouse and scenic stagecoach rides along the ocean road that traveled high up into the hills across the river. Between 1888 and 1890, expanded ferry service succeeded.

Chris Brenner's words resonate in the documentary *Destinations Past: Highland Beach*: "The railroad was actively involved in the construction of a railway bridge and a train station that satiated transportation needs of attendees from distant locations. On February 1, 1892, the Highland Beach Association sold to the Navesink Railroad Company a tract of land between Lots 33 and 37 for $1.00. A new bridge followed allowing the pedestrian and horse and carriage portion to remain with the construction of a new drawbridge."[17]

The resort acquired a legendary reputation when the numbers of visitors arriving from the cities increased. Tourism on the Jersey Shore awakened when other resorts arose and gained acclaim throughout the area. The *Oracle* newsletter at the resort reported that twenty-three yachts from the New York Association were received at the Highland Beach boathouse. A dance, illuminations, shooting gallery matches and prizes tempted the visitors. The 1892 Gala Day on the first Saturday of August was heavily promoted to increase resort business and showcase the tone and type of establishment. Over fifteen thousand visitors attended, including notable guests, who enjoyed regattas, prizes, contests and dances. According to contemporary accounts in the *Monmouth Press*, it was the "Leading Event of the Season at Highland Beach."[18] Throngs of beachgoers descended on the resort. Highland Beach advertisements widely circulated throughout New York City.

The year 1892 brought significant change. The Central Railroad of New Jersey's burgeoning growth gave rise to an idea. It added more rail lines crossing Monmouth County to increase capacity and built an enormous pier at Atlantic Highlands within three miles of the resort. This new construction allowed large steamboats from Manhattan to connect with the new rail line situated at the pier. Riders now had a choice of taking either the rail extension or a variety of smaller steam launches. The connecting rail line ran from the new pier in Atlantic Highlands to the newly finished criss-cross bridge at Highlands and Highland Beach. This new bridge also facilitated train, wagon and pedestrian traffic across the Shrewsbury. The old Highland Beach Station was moved south along the seawall to a spot that allowed the train tracks to curve onto the beach after coming across the river. The pedestrian and wagon span "criss-crossed" the train tracks and landed right in the middle of the resort at Highland Beach. Anticipating larger crowds, Highland Beach added one hundred bathhouses.

On a blistering hot day at the resort, a mirage was seen above the water. Spectators thought they saw a ship on fire. Other bathers saw a town in the hills and the harbor of New York in spectacular illumination. The wondrous sights continued for over an hour, fading in and out of sight, only to reappear in a more brilliant version. Once the cooler air arrived by the end of the day, the glorious apparitions evaporated. The phenomena are attributed to variations in temperature.

Above all, Will Sandlass was concerned with safety and to preserve the life of bathers at the resort. Will was proud to advertise that anyone swimming within the ropes of his establishment would be safe. The steamers continued to arrive filled to capacity on summer days, carrying up to 3,000 people a day. In 1892, the news exclaimed that Highland Beach had hosted over 125,000 visitors that summer, the largest numbers ever recorded at the resort up until that time.

The Fruit & Cigar Store/Sandlass residence on Surf Avenue, Highland Beach in 1893. William Sandlass and his mother, "Annie," are standing in the doorway. *Author's collection.*

In 1893, Will Sandlass moved forward with his enterprising spirit. A long boardwalk was added so that patrons could sit on the platform under a shaded area to enhance their comfort while looking out at the ocean. The Sandlass crew added more stores and buildings. The roller coaster ran its course when a patent infringement forced its removal as a major attraction after four years. Will constructed a Fruit & Cigar Store, as well as billiards and bowling venues, in place of the roller coaster near the seawall. The Sandlass family lived on the second floor above the store. Will's frugal and innovative nature as the son of a woodworker influenced his choice to build the house with the timbers of the roller coaster near its original footprint. The pot-bellied stove on the first floor of the Fruit & Cigar Store was a mainstay during the long winters. The family faced storms on the coast with only a sea wall for protection. On the right side of the store stood a great rock barrier, the only buffer for the advancing ocean waves during the perilous storms that rocked the seacoast. These boulders, stacked on top of each other, were designed to protect the New Jersey Southern Railroad's tracks running south to Long Branch. When summer arrived, Will encouraged his mother, Anna Elizabeth, to run the new store featuring "Annie's" fresh fruits at the first-floor entrance. On the hottest of summer days, homemade lemonade passed through these open windows to the thirsty bathers seeking some relief. Changes were planned for the coming year. The vanishing footprint of the former "Great Switchback" gravity railroad was about to usher in a new era. Will Sandlass also extended his lease with the Highland Beach Improvement Company for an additional five years. Effects of the earlier economic Panic of 1893 still reverberated around the country while enthusiasm for the resort jumped higher. On August 18, 1893, the *New York Times* raved about the experience of time spent in this popular vacation destination.

> *CAMPING ABOUT HIGHLAND BEACH:....Visitors have been treated to a peculiar sight during the past fortnight. Further down the beach toward Sandy Hook and situated under the rays of the famous twin Highland lights, is a large camping colony. The snow-white tents are situated on the riverside, a few feet back from high-water mark. In the rear of the tents, not far distant, splashes and roars from the surf of the Atlantic. This camping idea is becoming a popular fad here, and people from New York, Paterson, Brooklyn, Jersey City, and near-by towns take this method to spend a few pleasurable weeks during the heated term.*[19]

By 1894, Will had added another three hundred bathhouses to the expanding establishment. At least five hundred bathhouses were ready to accommodate visitors buying day passes at the Bathing Pavilion windows. In August 1894, the *Monmouth Press* reported the well-established yearly event in August a resounding success:

> *GALA DAY AT HIGHLAND BEACH....To-day is gala day at Highland Beach. While on former occasions the day has been one full of enjoyment this year promises to be far in advance of all others. The morning and afternoon will be devoted to bicycle races, running races, launch and yacht races, swimming, rowing, etc. And in the evening will occur the marine review, etc. A hop at the Surf House, given by Mr. Sandlass, also is one of the attractions. Everyone who has visited this beautiful resort knows that the occasion will prove one of the pleasantest and most successful events of the season.*[20]

The golden age of Highland Beach had arrived!

PART III

Improvement Meets Growth

1894–1898

At Highland Beach, with its swimming, boating, switch-back roller coaster and carousel, there seemed to be no limit to the sun and fun. At the tip of Sandy Hook, however, was a reminder that the world was also getting smaller. Fort Hancock boasted the nation's most sophisticated harbor defenses, and later served as a proving ground for some of the world's most powerful weapons of war.

—Mark Stewart, quoted in an exhibit showcasing Highland Beach legends and artifacts at the Twin Lights Museum

Bathers at Highland Beach excursion resort enjoying a day of leisure, circa 1890s. *Author's collection.*

10

GROWTH OF THE MIDDLE CLASS

As 1894 was ushered in, economic ramifications prevailed from the previous year at the resort. At the same time, the new era of leisure time manifested itself in the increased spending of the emerging middle class. The U.S. economy rose at the fastest rate in its history from the 1870s through the 1890s, while two major nationwide depressions known as the Panic of 1873 and the Panic of 1893 interrupted growth. The latter panic affected the Sandy Hook real estate development plans by local investors and altered the nature of building on the southern end of the Sandy Hook peninsula. There was also much social conflict. American wages, higher than in Europe, attracted millions of immigrants. The wave of immigration and European values impacted life throughout the nation. Immigrants provided a workforce to power the new factories and industries of cities.

This period coincided with the Gilded Age of the United States (1860s–1896). The term *Gilded Age* was coined by Mark Twain and Charles Dudley Warner in *The Gilded Age: A Tale of Today*, published in 1873 as a satire that highlighted social problems disguised by "a thin gold gilding." Prohibition and foreign-language schools (German Catholic and Lutheran) were hard-fought political issues of the times. Being of stout German heritage and the son of immigrants, Will and his family were affected by the social norms. The middle class arose amid these social and economic conflicts. Larger incomes and more leisure time among these workers advanced the idea of purchasing and using goods and services and fostered popular amusements in American cities. Jobs in the cities were demanding, and housing conditions

Ocean bathing at Highland Beach, New Jersey. *Author's collection.*

were crowded and unsanitary for most of these workers. This new era was filled with opportunity and saw innovation in industry. It produced openings for clerical jobs that promoted the development of the middle class. Male and female office workers had money to spend on a variety of goods for consumption and free time to enjoy activities. This newly established culture fueled the revenues of the resort. Highland Beach was a perfect site to answer the needs of an emerging population in the Gilded Age. Wisconsin-born author Thorstein Veblen argued in his book *The Theory of the Leisure Class* that the "conspicuous consumption and conspicuous leisure"[21] of the wealthy and the middle class had become the basis of social status in America. The Victorian years witnessed an ever-increasing appetite for recreation and entertainment. As a new century approached, the Edwardians reached for modernity. This golden age would be known for its pursuit of pleasure. Highland Beach readied itself to deliver the most pleasing of memories.

11

STORMS PREVAIL

Storms along the coast became a way of life at the resort. Another savage gale was on the horizon during the morning of April 11, 1894. When the *Kate Markee*, a three-masted schooner loaded with paving stones, wrecked on Highland Beach, Sandy Hook and Sea Bright lifesaving crews rushed out to the scene. These valiant men were unable to save a single man of the eight on the vessel. The hurricane force of rain, snow and wind lashed out from the heavy sea, and the rescuers were unable to get lines to the ship. The storm washed away the railroad track between Highland Beach and Sea Bright. At least one cottage owned by Mr. Earle near the Normandie By the Sea hotel was undermined. Paving stones and wood from the wreckage washed up on the shores of Highland Beach and Sandy Hook. That summer, fishermen in a squatter's village between Highland Beach and Fort Hancock devised makeshift homes with the remnants of the wreck. The men were eventually evicted by the military. The following year, piledrivers worked diligently building a trestle for the government tracks at Highland Beach. The storms on Sandy Hook repeatedly washed out the track. Building a trestle allowed the sea to wash under it without carrying the track into the river.

When the summer of 1894 arrived, the newspapers were ready to report more Camp Comfort news about this sandy strip below the lush green hills of Highlands. On August 22, 1894, the *Red Bank Register* article broadcasted more excitement for this new vacation spot.

CAMP COMFORT: A Bright Story of Camp Life on the Beach. Uncle Sam has always been noted for his hospitality and good will, and people who happen to know his disposition have availed themselves of the opportunity this summer and camped below the proving ground at Sandy Hook, on a narrow strip of sand beach which is not of much use for Uncle Sam's purposes.

If one lands at Highland Beach and walks a short distance down the railroad that runs to Sandy Hook he will see a big sign on a telegraph pole, "U.S. Reservation; no trespassing under penalty of the law," and directly underneath this sign is a tent which is the first one of a stretch of tents for half a mile down the beach. The tents face the Shrewsbury river and at a very high tide one can see the spray dashing up on the ocean side. Here the occupants of "Camp Comfort" have enjoyed themselves for a week. Atlantic Highlands, with its railroad, a perfect imitation of the Hudson scenery; the beautiful Shrewsbury with its numerous craft, the white sand of Sandy Hook, and the ever-restless ocean form a picture of constant change.

At night the twin lights on the Highlands shine far out at sea, guiding and making safe the mariner. All day long the traffic up and down the Shrewsbury makes the front yards of the campers very lively. The campers get out on the beach and as each boat passes with its load of passengers and freight, give the camp call, wave a flag, or blow a horn from "Hornville Camp." Here, "Angler's Rest" affords a pleasant home for a party who are fond of fishing. "Laurel" floats a blue pennant with the name of the tent on it. The occupants of the tent probably have earned their laurels and have come to rest.

During the past week a red and white flag has attracted much attention. A white cross runs lengthwise through the flag, the initial letters of the words "Red Bank Trinity Church Choir" standing in the four corners….

Next door to "Camp Comfort" stands a fisherman's home. The house is built of the wreckage of the Nicol, the tug that went down in a squall not many weeks ago. It is not very beautiful, looks like a "Black Maria," [paddy wagon] *for it is covered with tar paper and tin-headed nails. The occupants are four or five fishermen….*

But just step inside of this adjoining cottage. This place, he said, "is built from the timber of the Kate Markee, the three-masted schooner that went down last spring." Then we went up three steps (for this little dwelling is built on a float,) and looked in the door…There were a cooking stove, two chairs, dishes, a lantern, and everything complete to keep house with. "Sea Shell" as the house is called is anchored now, but it is all ready, in

> *case of a bad storm, to pull up anchor and float, like Noah's ark, until the flood goes down.*
>
> *Another interesting feature of Sandy Hook is watching the cannon balls as they shoot out at sea.... These are a very few (items) of interest that have come under "Camp Comfort's" observation.*[22]

Camp Comfort's favorite vacation spot on this beach belonged to the military. There was a distance of a few miles between the campers and the military reservation. No boundary line existed in 1894 in this location to indicate the U.S. Army's first proving ground for the testing of ordnance (guns and artillery) at the far end of Sandy Hook. The military took exception to the squatters in temporary dwellings and evicted the "eyesore" next to the resort as reported in the local news. The popular trend of camping in tents continued to grow in the Highlands area, expanding the summer population. Just over two weeks in July, eight excursions arrived, including a big trainload of excursionists from Newark, one from Lakewood and a Sunday crowd brought down to the resort by regular boats. When the third week of June arrived, the excursions ranged from six hundred to eight hundred people, represented by desirable groups such as Sunday schools, churches, lodges and societies. The season was nearly at its height in the busy month of August.

Highland Beach pier, where local steamboats brought excursionists to the resort. *Author's collection.*

The resort management built a pier as part of the improvements that year. Several trips were made daily, including Sundays, by steamers between New York and Highland Beach. The investment in building a pier added greatly to the number of visitors. It cost fifty cents (fourteen dollars in 2019) for round-trip passengers to travel on the *Sea Bird* and *Albertina*. Picnic parties multiplied as transportation availability opened up. A well-patronized Surf House and Bathing Pavilion gave the management at Highland Beach cause for a happy outlook that season. The *Monmouth Press* reported on September 15, 1894:

> *Highland Beach Flourishing Also.... The largest excursions ever entertained at this queen of excursion resorts came this summer and more of them. The excellent boarding season at the Highlands of Navesink and Atlantic Highlands ensured the bathing pavilion unusual patronage. The direct steamers to New York from the wharf here have brought many parties.*
>
> *Altogether the place is booming. So much so that the management has ordered the erection of 200 new bath houses, extending the group northward considerably. The houses are of large size like the others. A new gate house on a more pretentious scale has been erected with a capacity equal for the hundreds more keys and towels needful to be handled with enlarged facilities.*
>
> *There are a number of pleasant improvements in progress at the ladies dressing room. It will be twice as large in the first place. Then another season will find Brussels carpets and handsome furnishings there with a matron-in-charge. A hair dressing establishment is to be opened in connection with the dressing room in deference to popular demand.*
>
> *Landlord Sandlass wears a smiling face. His guests have almost all gone. But he possesses evidences in his bank account of their presence in gratifying numbers.*
>
> *The season is not over. Indeed, President Fish threatens to prolong it till the river freezes over, so well does business continue. No guests are to be driven away through neglect of the Improvement Company.*[23]

Increased traffic congestion on Ocean Avenue was the main concern. Ferdinand Fish sold the turnpike road between Highland Beach and Sea Bright to new owners from Sea Bright, Highlands and Rumson Neck to prevent a trolley road from being constructed. The Cottage Colony at Navesink Beach, comprising seaside mansions, continued to grow in tandem with the resort on the peninsula. Ferdinand Fish, the selling agent for the Navesink Beach Cottages adjacent to Highland Beach, rapidly filled the homes in the summer of 1894. A list of well-known names of the day occupied these seaside cottages. The *Oracle* resort newsletter reported that Fish would begin construction of a house to cost $3,000 ($84,000 in 2019 terms) from plans by C.W. Humphreys, his architect son-in-law. He expanded his real estate interests in 1894 when a group of New York architects became interested in undertaking development of a large tract of land located in the Highlands hillside. They joined together to form the Water Witch Club Park (named from an 1830 novel written by James Fenimore Cooper, *The Water-Witch: The Skimmer of the Seas*, a smuggling tale partially set in the rough waters of Sandy Hook Bay).[24] A limited membership was offered with the intention of creating a parklike setting called Monmouth Hills. Ferdinand Fish, the first president, and members adopted bylaws and elected their first officers in a meeting at the Highland Beach Surf House.

Just at the edge of Sea Bright, the nearby town of Monmouth Beach was known for having a summer "Cottage" every two hundred yards. The gambling that accompanied the races at Monmouth Park drew the sporting crowd to Long Branch. The main artery, Ocean Avenue, was little more than a dirt road. More hotels sprang up to serve the new clientele, who were in search of grander accommodations. In Dominick Mazzagetti's *The Jersey Shore,* he notes that Asbury Park's founder, James Bradley, a driving force in the town's founding and one of the faithful from Ocean Grove, was a strong opponent of horse-race gambling. He tried to put his moral stamp on the community by supporting legislation that led to the loss of racing at Monmouth Park in 1894 and eliminated this as an advantage for the rival town of Long Branch. Monmouth Park's owners struggled to stay afloat by offering the property as a fairground location.[25]

12

"GALA DAYS" REAP REWARDS

The Highland Beach Improvement Company published its *Oracle* subscription newsletter to keep the latest news in front of its most ardent members and guests, who filled their social clubs, "Cottages" and the Bathing Pavilion. A memorable affair took place on a balmy day on the river side of Highland Beach when the signature event of the season, the fourth Gala Day celebration, was held in August 1894. Guests found an array of choices on their arrival: rowing races, regatta competitions, fishing contests, auto-boat races, diving contests, boat parades and an evening dance with "Grand Illuminations" (fireworks) to light up the night sky. Local newspapers covered the event, noting with excitement the enormous crowds of five thousand or more attending in one day. Dignitaries and celebrities joined in the fun each successive year. They included visitors from the New York Yacht Club; the ex-mayor of Cincinnati, William Means; and the New Jersey governor, Robert Green. The *Monmouth Press* on August 18, 1894, reported:

> *Fully 5,000 people crowded every inch of space. The bridge was a compact mass of humanity. The steamboat wharf was jammed and the river bank was black with people. While never before were so many craft of every description crowded into so small a space on the river....The enthusiasm was simply intense. The clanging of the boathouse bell, the incessant firing of cannon from many yachts, salutes of steam whistles from passing excursion or pleasure boats and the vociferous cheering of the crowds as one*

The fourth Gala Day celebration at Highland Beach with Grand Illumination, Marine Parade and a Hop in the Evening. *Author's collection.*

> *after another of the many contests were finished, made the scene one long to be remembered.*[26]

Friendly rivalries existed between some of the boats in the races, creating a lot of interest. The first prize for the best-decorated rowboat or canoe went to Anna L. Fish, Ferdinand Fish's daughter. Her canoe, *The Lohengrin*, was named after a romantic opera by Richard Wagner inspired by the epic Knight of the Swan legend. She held forth in grand style. The boat was trimmed with laurel from bow to stern and featured a large Chinese umbrella suspended above. Chinese lanterns and yellow material completed the design. Anna Fish reclined against red and yellow cushions and burned colored fire reflected in the lanterns. A four-foot swan adorned the bow. From all accounts, the crowd was enchanted. For her effort, she received a first-prize marine painting by James Buttersworth, a celebrated artist of the day.

As anticipation grew at Gala Day, awards took center stage. Safety being a key priority for Sandlass, the lifesaving medal for five years of service was presented to Harry Meares. He had saved the lives of over one hundred endangered swimmers, despite ropes being placed in the water for swimmers to hold on to for safety. While they were sea bathing, waves would often unexpectedly carry swimmers away. Even the shooting gallery offered prizes earned during the summer season and were awarded on Gala Day. This notable day showcased for the crowd a river filled with regatta yachts. One yacht in particular, *Linda*, commanded attention on the water. By all reports, it was the grandest of private yachts.

Excitement grew when a bicycle race was contested after protests erupted. One cyclist was thought to be a professional. On further investigation, he was confirmed as a prizewinning amateur. The race was one mile in length from flagpole to Normandie and could be completed in twelve minutes. Back on the river, the four-oared crew race ended in a dead heat in the time of one minute, seven seconds. A few of the prizes included a scallop shell in gold with the figure of a diver in silver and a jeweled medal given for swimming. At the end of the day, Will Sandlass gave a "hop" at the Surf House. Ragtime and Tin Pan Alley music had gained in popularity from the 1880s and reached its height in 1899. One of the most popular groups of musicians in New York City, Earl Fuller's Famous Jazz Band, traveled to the shore from Rector's highly fashionable restaurant on Broadway, a place where diners went to "see and be seen." On the special nights at Sandlass Pavilion, Fuller's jazz band played to the crowds during the craze of the turkey trot, fish walk and bunny hug. The crowds grew to fifteen thousand as the Gala Day event gained in popularity.

Despite all the fun at Gala Day, the effect of the earlier economic panic was not the only thing to worry about at Highland Beach. In his *Destinations Past: Highland Beach* documentary, Chris Brenner says: "The morals of the era leaned toward civility and religious respect, and public sentiment started to question games of chance and alcohol consumption as corruptive forces in society, and local laws were passed prohibiting some of the games and attractions from operation on Sundays which was one of the biggest days of the week. One account has the local constable demanding Sandlass shut down the carousel on Sundays."[27]

The ornately carved animals with flying manes held memories of magical childhood moments perched atop a fiery steed while whirling to the music of the carousel. The resort business surmounted this latest barrier and continued to be a favorite destination for excursionists visiting the shore. The *Red Bank Daily Register* in 1895 picked up the news about blue laws (preventing entertainment or leisure activities on Sundays) being enforced in New York City. A great exodus to Coney Island and other resorts meant a benefit for Highland Beach, which got its full share of the exodus. The *Monmouth Press* reported in 1895: "Since the enforcement of the Sunday laws in New York,

THE ORACLE OF THE HIGHLANDS OF NAVESINK

Vol. 1. HIGHLAND BEACH, N. J., FEBRUARY, 1896. No. 9.

GENERAL VIEW OF THE HIGHLANDS OF NAVESINK AND WATER-WITCH PARK (FROM HIGHLAND BEACH).

The *Highland Beach Oracle* newsletter gave subscribers a peek into resort life in February 1896. *Courtesy of John King's collection.*

Highland Beach has become a great Sunday resort. Crowds visited the sandy stretch last Sunday. It is said Red Bankers spend more money at Highland Beach than people from the cities."[28]

Sandlass Pavilion at Highland Beach immediately benefited from the new rail connection originating at the Atlantic Highlands pier. Since the railroad crossed the river, summer visitors encountered this new seaside resort on the rail journey from local towns heading toward the coastline. Lazy days among the houseboats, tents and bungalows afforded a perfect rendezvous for anyone wishing to get away from the heat and hectic pace. Power yachts and canoes cruised the shores by the scrub marshes filled with nature's wildlife, providing ample room to make this one of the most popular resorts of its day.

Highlands had acquired a new train station. Even so, there was something missing. It had hotels, steamboat docks (with the Merchant and Patten lines making several stops a day), boardinghouses, bars and the famous Twin Lights attraction, but no ocean bathing and no boardwalk. Even though Highland Beach had one hotel, it, too, lacked something. The large number of hotels, boardinghouse accommodations and bars were across the bridge in Highlands. A symbiotic relationship developed between the town of Highlands and Highland Beach. William Sandlass's Highland Beach excursion resort was decidedly one of the several elements that influenced the successful development of Highlands as a major tourist destination, mentioned by John King in his book *Highlands, New Jersey*.[29]

Tents continued to rise in even greater numbers. Vacationers in search of affordable housing continued to look for respite from the dog days of summer. Many encampments reflecting the popularity of Highlands and Highland Beach proliferated along the riverbanks and sandy shores of the nearby coves on the peninsula.

In 1895, Fish leased property opposite the railroad station at the Highlands of Navesink. Within a year, there was difficulty in getting permission to bring water to the hillside community at Water Witch. The group forged ahead with a campaign offering a house design competition in the Highland Beach *Oracle* newsletter to foster enthusiasm for the project. A clubhouse and cottages were part of the enterprise, similar to the aristocratic Twilight Park in the Catskill Mountains. Fish experienced financial challenges and partnership disagreements during the Water Witch Park venture. This eventually led him to withdraw from the endeavor, leaving his partners to complete the development of the project. The Monmouth Hills community and its clubhouse, the Water Witch Casino near the Twin lighthouses in the Highlands of Navesink, evolved into a historically important community. Fish's financial fortunes declined over the next few years, leading him to give up his influence on the future of Highland Beach. He was considered one of the driving forces at the outset of the nineteenth-century communities on the northernmost point of the Jersey Shore, including Highland Beach, Navesink Beach, Monmouth Hills and Water Witch Casino (historic site), as well as Hilton (Atlantic Highlands).

In the greater context, the magnitude of the Highland Beach resort's popularity continued to have an enormous impact on the southern end of the Sandy Hook peninsula and neighboring resort towns. The reach of the resort touched the towns of Highlands, Sea Bright, Rumson, Monmouth Beach and Long Branch over the history of its presence on the peninsula. This seashore location slept from October to May and awoke again each summer. The 1895 *Standard Union* newspaper of Brooklyn reminds us: "The air of stillness awakened each summer when cottage life was filled with guests that arrived from New York. Trunks and traps moved oceanward on the rail cars owned by The Central Railroad of New Jersey. Sandy Hook boats from Pier 8, North River, did a very large business offering a pleasant trip to the seashore. Visitors found that the fisherman's colony of Sea Bright attracted the curiosity of many strangers in town."[30]

13

NEW ATTRACTIONS

When local seaside towns came to life, they brought out the stars as soon as the warm weather arrived, filling up the beach communities with all levels of society. The entertainments advertised at the resort reflected a period when the Elegant Eighties transitioned into the golden decade of the Gay Nineties, a time of high living and big spenders. The actors' colony grew to include filmmakers attracted to this location at the beach. As the summers unfolded, some of the entertainers, including Broadway actor Thomas Q. Seabrooke and writer Charles Byrnes of New York City, were guests at the Highland Beach Surf House.

Riverboats awaited the latest trends in transportation to increase their passenger rolls. The steamers *Sea Bird* and *Albertina* docked first at Highland Beach before crossing to Highlands. Before the advent of the motorcar, the electric trolley replaced the stagecoach to some degree. The routes traveled from Atlantic Highlands to Highlands, Keyport to Highlands and Middletown to Highlands, where the steamboats connected to the trolley at Highlands. A small *Highland Beach* catamaran was launched in the summer of 1895. It made two trips daily on weekends and three on Sundays and holidays between Red Bank and the Highlands. As a youth, historian Leon Reussille took many a Sunday trip on the little catamaran. He shared his memories of those trips in his writings, mentioning that most aboard would cross the bridge to Highland Beach, arms filled with picnic baskets, heading to the Sandlass Pavilion overlooking the river. Just below the pavilion were the bathhouses and the river bathing beach with its large float for sunning

"Viewing Highland Beach," a postcard of the popular river bathing on a moonlit evening at the turn of the twentieth century. *Courtesy of John King's collection.*

and diving. A few steps away to the east was a narrow neck of land where they enjoyed ocean bathing.[31]

Two additional fast steamers were built to go to Highland Beach in the summer of 1895. The direct local service brought greater numbers to attend the resort. The *Jersey Lily*, *Our Mary*, *Leon Abbett*, *Highland Beach*, *Shrewsbury* and *Navesink* plied the rivers that summer. When the full complement of six steamers made seven round trips each summer, they brought 3,000 persons a day! The Highlands hotels thrived across the river. An attempt was made by the Highland Beach Improvement Company to purchase Thompson's Pavilion, the East View House and Swift's Pavilion in anticipation of the resort growth. The steamers *Shrewsbury* and *Navesink* were put into service on July 2, accommodating 500 passengers a day from Red Bank to Highland Beach. There was a nominal fee for the forty-five-minute trip, with extra attractions at night offering "moonlight" excursions for twenty-five cents.

Day fares remained at ten cents for one-way trips. The boats made several trips a day with a 128-passenger capacity and an extra trip at night on Sundays. The waters were shallow in certain locations at the resort, causing one of the steamers to hit something below the waterline. The *Shrewsbury* steamer struck a submerged obstacle and broke one of its propeller blades. Once the damaged steamer was repaired, sale of the riverboats was made to the Spanish Consul for $10,000 (equivalent to $291,000 in 2019). At the end of the summer, after just one month of service on the Shrewsbury River, the riverboat sale included the *Shrewsbury*, the *Navesink* and the *Leon Abbet* steamers. (They were delivered by steamer to Havana and used during the revolution in Cuban waters for boarding launches to transfer soldiers from one boat to another. Ultimately, the United States severed ties with Spain during the Spanish-American War in 1898.)

The unpredictable weather always brought a concern around the biggest day of the year. Thousands of dollars were lost to Highland Beach on one of the Fourth of July weekends as a result of dismal weather. The *Oracle* newsletter reported that the crowd could scarcely leave the rail cars due to the exceptional downpour. The cool weather that continued did not favor excursions until the cool spell broke the following week. Mother nature finally cooperated. The biggest excursion of the season arrived the following Thursday. The Merry-Go-Round was full, the Rifle Gallery had many patrons and the restaurants did a "rushing" business, in which one could buy refreshments other than lemonade and ginger pop. The Bathing Pavilion filled up with patrons and ruled the day when bathers crowded both the ocean and river beaches. The *Oracle* shared an amusing story about a little girl who approached the Bathing Pavilion window with a question. There was a sign posted for the benefit of patrons that said, "Look out for thieves!" After reading the sign, the little girl asked, "Can I see the thieves?"[32]

In the summer of 1895, media coverage of the America's Cup race at Sandy Hook gave visitors a front-row seat in the shadow of Highland Beach over several days. Watching the trial yacht race between the *Defender* and the *Vigilant* (the 1893 winner), both representing the United States, brought people by trains, wagons, bicycles and riverboats. The hazy weather obscured the race most of the day until the very end, when the yachts came into sight. Even so, the *New York World* newspaper's hot-air balloon entertained the spectators while they waited for the yachts to appear. The balloon was a sensation that ultimately fizzled. Onlookers had to give the balloon an assist to get it off the ground to rise at all. Two-thirds of the race was taken up with the aborted balloon launch when the fog lifted, and the onlookers

Highland Beach, Sandy Hook. The hot-air balloon attraction advertised the America's Cup Race, 1895. *Courtesy of the* Evening World *archives.*

rushed to see the end of the race. The crowd was made up almost entirely of summer visitors. The ultimate winner of the 1895 America's Cup was the *Defender* (New York Yacht Club), which raced against *Valkyrie III* (Royal Yacht Squadron, United Kingdom), winning a best-of-five regatta.

In September 1895, the boardwalk was taken up, buildings were closed and most cottagers went home. Will Sandlass made the decision to move Catherine and their ten-year old son, Bill, from New York City to the shore. The family would now live year-round in the Highland Beach residence above the Fruit & Cigar Store so that he could work on the resort's facilities in the off-season. Will spent his time as a carpenter and decided to form a construction company, thus becoming part of the local economy year-round. The company made him available for contractual work in the area.

This type of work also allowed him to make his own improvements at the Sandlass Pavilion.

The new season opened on Decoration Day, May 25, 1896. All of the buildings were renewed with fresh paint, ornamental work and a unique rustic fence surrounding the large Sandlass Pavilion. The Highland Beach Bowling Club was in full practice at Sandlass's regulation alleys, pronounced equal to any in the state, and proposed to challenge all clubs in the county. The *Monmouth Press* reported on June 6, 1896:

> *At Highland Beach, Wm. Sandlass, Jr. has added largely to the many attractions of his place. A unique rustic fence now surrounds his roomy and airy pavilion. The lawns and shrubbery are beyond comparison. He has ten excursions booked from Newark, and numbers more from New Brunswick, Jersey City and from other New Jersey cities and towns and a lot from New York and Brooklyn. The main attractions are the four "B's"—boating, bathing, bowling and billiards. Johnson Sandlass arrived from Baltimore recently and will assist his brother in the summer management.*
>
> *The pounding breakers of the Atlantic rise up—the real surf gives summer visitors exceptional advantages for short outings at Highland Beach with all the advertised excitement of amenities for food, lodging, games and fun.*[33]

Everything was in full blast. Highland Beach Improvement Company announced in the *Oracle* newsletter that bathing at Highland Beach was the finest on the coast north of Cape May. It advertised that twenty furnished private dressing rooms were added on the second floor of the Bathing Pavilion for those who preferred more privacy. Reservations cost two dollars a week. The Photography Gallery, under the direction of Mr. Vantine, offered a memory in one of the Highland Beach (HB) monogramed bathing suits for twenty-five cents. Mr. C.E. Overbaugh (crack shot) ran the shooting gallery. "No bar goods (beer or sub-par liquor) were on the premises…only the finest wines and liquors were in stock." Special inducements were offered to excursionists to make their headquarters at Sandlass Pavilion. With the addition of a model kitchen, the Surf House was greatly enlarged and improved. The Basket Pavilion accommodated one thousand people a day in three sittings. Basket parties were offered at reasonable prices under the always cool and big shady roof. Dancing and an orchestra delighted the patrons at the pavilion day and night.

The bicycle craze was in high gear at the shore. Highland Beach responded to the trend. A local shop leased the ground between the Photo Gallery and the Merry-Go-Round to build a bicycle rest as a great convenience for thousands of seasonal cyclers who made Highland Beach a destination. The bike shack had full-time employees who were available to rent, repair or store bikes. Bike races were a regular attraction in the summer. Over three years, Asbury Park held bicycle races at the local stadium and provided a bicycle path along the ocean road. Summer baby parades in Asbury Park were a major attraction. The success of these parades motivated local towns to follow suit with parades at several Monmouth County resorts. The seaside community of Asbury Park in Monmouth County, New Jersey, drew such large crowds that it was deemed the biggest resort at the time.

The calls continued to arrive for advance excursion bookings at Highland Beach. The New York YMCA (all divisions) was one of the many organizations to enjoy all the amenities that unfolded at the resort. The company newsletter advertised the Tom Swift as the best hotel in Highlands while enjoying one's stay at the shore. A sandbar near the stable had been built out nearly fifty feet, causing steamers to have difficulty going around the bridge. It necessitated the building of a seventy-five-foot extension to the Highland Beach pier in the river. All was not perfect during that summer season. The remnants of the recent economic panic still showed its effects, as reported in the *Oracle*: "The poverty of the people could still be felt and reduced the number of excursionists."[34] The same issue reported rumors of malaria that scared people away earlier than usual from the west end of the Highlands Bridge. Nevertheless, Will Sandlass was kept busy answering letters from clubs and societies asking for accommodations at the beach. Highland Beach neared the end of its summer season taking pride in the attention it gave to the activities offered to guests. The St. Lawrence River canoes were still in good condition by the end of the season. Will took extra care with his equipment and facilities to keep maintenance costs down. As summer drew to a close and crowds dwindled, a "To Let" sign was posted on the stable near the dock due to lack of demand for livery. It was offered as a casino site, and within a short time, the Mel-Rah Club was born. The casino (social club) was the predecessor of two more clubs (Dar-He and Surf Clubs) that opened at the resort in the coming years.

A severe storm hit the coast late in the season in October 1896, bringing the Sea Bright and Sandy Hook area to its knees. An inlet was made at Highland Beach north of the stable near Island Beach (Plum Island), while the bathhouses at the north end of the Bathing Pavilion were carried away. Bulkheads and cottages were damaged over three days as the storm battered the coast. Government telephone and telegraph lines were broken down, railroad tracks were covered with three feet of sand and the ocean washed over the beach where the river met the ocean in the middle. Most of the docks and boats, secured for protection from the storm, were underwater. Danger of the inlet remaining open was dismissed, as the west wind always brought sand to fill it up again. Once again, the forces of nature required Will to face the inevitable challenges wrought on the coastline. A winter spent rebuilding the infrastructure of the resort began when the weather cleared. In spite of the setbacks from major storm damage, the resort continued to thrive.

By 1897, Will Sandlass had proven the resort was a success. His profitability put him in a stronger position when he signed a new twenty-five-year lease in a land transfer with the Highland Beach Improvement Company. He could now guarantee a future generation "summers of fun" at the resort. Will estimated the expense of his improvements at $7,000 (equal to $209,000 in 2019). They were intended to give guests a more pleasant welcome. It included a new pier and a new seawall, and buildings were moved. The Sandlass Pavilion at Highland Beach surrounded its guests daily with a wide variety of diversions. Will had operators overseeing the daily work at the Merry-Go-Round (Harry Semler), Popcorn Man (Mr. S.S. Sagues), the Photography Studio (Henry Vantine), the Surf House (Conrad Stein), the Basket Pavilion (Frank Worrell, chef), the Bathing Pavilion (Mr. Hayward, general manager) and the other amusement areas. Leasing out the attractions gave Will time to orchestrate a favorable environment to draw the large crowds that descended on the resort. These new attractions were attended by a staff whose experience and courtesy contributed to the comfort of the guests. By all accounts, Will ensured that each staff member was of equal importance in serving the needs of visitors to the resort. The *Monmouth Press* covered the happenings at Highland Beach every summer as it grew in renown. Cashier H.V. Bittings was at his job over four years, and Philip Lynch fitted his "fat and lean, great and small fellow citizens in bathing suits," always ready to serve again. Lifesavers contributed to the proud record of saving lives in the tempestuous waters. Known for their lifesaving skills, Harry Meares, Percy Magronigle and W.D. Emery, assisted by Mr. Lynch, averted tragedy when they rescued a Mr. J.W. Bolen and his wife from the waves in a hailstorm as their yacht capsized near the bathing grounds. A common practice rewarded the lifesavers with collected funds to compliment them for their bravery.[35]

Living by the water's edge provided Will with the opportunity for relaxation when the resort closed at the end of the day. The Highlands Bridge was widely known as the best fishing spot in the area. The *Red Bank Register* of

May 19, 1897, reported, "The first haddock ever known to have been caught in the Shrewsbury river was caught last week by William Sandlass proprietor of Highland Beach grounds. The fish weighed 9½ pounds."[36]

A dispute arose in 1897 over contested public lands on the river at Highland Beach. The confrontation with the freeholders revolved around the title for the previous purchase of the Highlands Bridge by the county. The Highland Beach Association had the Surf House and other buildings on the land at the time of the bridge purchase. The freeholders wanted the Highland Beach Association to move off the land or charge them a rental fee. A search of the records by the county's legal counsel uncovered a previous claim and settlement on behalf of Highland Beach. It resolved the threat to the land and declared it legally part of the Highland Beach deed of ownership.

A new century of movies appeared on the horizon when the silent-film era was ushered in along the coast at Highlands and Highland Beach. The great innovative motion picture director D.W. Griffith came to nearby beaches at the turn of the century. In an article, John King noted that the first films made by the American Mutoscope Company were military in nature: *Projectile from Ten Inch Disappearing Gun Striking Water, Sandy Hook* was shot at the Proving Grounds at Fort Hancock in 1897 and the *Spanish Battleship Viscaya* off Sandy Hook in February 1898.[37] The year ended with transportation to the resort at its height, bringing the largest number of visitors in its history. Steamboats, trains, carriages and walking traffic from Highlands boosted revenue to meet the demands of ever-increasing tourists.

PART IV

Auto Age Begins

1898–1912

As the new decade of 1910 arrived, so did the first sightings of a new and life changing device—the automobile. Up until this point, visitors to Highland Beach arrived by train or boat, and destinations were limited to locations serviced by mass transportation, or limited by the duration of a buggy ride. With the advent of the car, things started to change. The first challenge for Sandlass was how to provide parking on a strip of land so narrow it barely held the pedestrians during busy weekends. As roadways improved, so did the traffic, and what started in this decade would prove to foreshadow bigger challenges in the future. With all three modes of transportation in use during 1910, it was, in fact the busiest summer ever at the resort.

—Chris Brenner

Sunday morning at Highland Beach. The auto age impacted the excursion resort served by trains and steamboats, as a result of limited parking space. *Author's collection.*

14

AMERICA'S CUP SPURS HEYDAY

A day at Highland Beach excursion resort was a unique experience, publicized in commercial picture postcards as the "first bathing resort on the Jersey Shore, located on the Sandy Hook Peninsula." Highland Beach and its place on the peninsula were described in an article at the Monmouth County Archives:

> *Highland Beach.... This may well be called the outpost of the Government fortifications and proving grounds on the peninsula, the northerly tip of which is universally known as Sandy Hook; it is here that the railroad spur under Army operation links the reservation with the outside world.*
>
> *Here, also, the summer visitor finds first access to the real surf—the pounding breakers of the Atlantic. At this point the Shrewsbury veers its northerly course to the eastward, and again to the north, where it broadens into Sandy Hook Bay; thus Highland Beach has water on three sides, while the terrain to the south is only a few rods in width....*
>
> *Aside from the attractions for permanent sojourners, Highland Beach, with its exceptional advantages for short outings, is one of the most popular resorts for day excursionists in the metropolitan district.*[38]

Growth and success continued with such high points as the tenth challenge for the America's Cup. In view of the racecourse, the America's Cup committee selected this coastline as the site for the international sport. The *New York Times* related on June 10, 1899:

The *Shamrock* and the *Columbia*, America's Cup Race, 1899 at Sandy Hook. *Courtesy of the Cosgrove/Bahrs collection.*

> *SELECT RACE DATES FOR AMERICA'S CUP, DEFENDER AND CHALLENGER TO RACE OFF SANDY HOOK ON SEPT. 10, 12 AND 15. The sky, which had been cloudy all day, had cleared toward sundown, and the Columbia went overboard with the stars feebly fighting to illuminate her amid a great glare of calcium lights. The launching was perfect in all its arrangements and was marred only by an accident caused by the wild eagerness of a photographer to get a flash-light picture.... This incident was unknown to the mass of spectators.... The north pier had been thrown open to the public, and every available space was occupied...the big white hull could be seen slowly descending. Applause and cheers at once rent the air. Mrs. Iselin dashed the bottle of champagne against the yacht's bow, saying, "I christen thee Columbia." As soon as the mast step was clear a staff was set up in it, carrying the private signals of J. Pierpont Morgan and C. Oliver Iselin, and when the bow appeared the New York Yacht Club flag was set up there. The yacht's bow was draped with festoons of flowers running from the stern to hawse pipes.*[39]

The grandeur of prestigious sloops in full sail could be seen by the crowd just below the tip of Sandy Hook on September 10, 1899. A day later, a storm, at times approaching hurricane velocity, caused considerable damage to several of the nearby towns. At Highlands, several houses were blown down and Sandlass' Surf House hotel suffered a great deal of damage. Preparation for the coming race was delayed two weeks into October because of weather conditions.

The America's Cup, started in 1851, is the oldest active trophy in international sport, awarded to the winner of match races between two yachts. In 1899, the America's Cup competitive climate was estranged. A Scottish businessman, Sir Thomas Lipton, became the financial backer of the Royal Ulster Yacht Club's challenge. Because of past success in American waters, William Fife was chosen as the designer of the challenging yacht, the *Shamrock*. The yachts increased in size that year, and the defender, *Columbia*, was fitted with a telescopic steel mast. Charlie Barr was chosen as the Scottish American skipper. He skippered Fife's designs in the past and had great confidence in his Scandinavian crew. The *Columbia*, was entered by the New York Yacht Club, and Sir Thomas Lipton's *Shamrock* represented the Royal Ulster Yacht Club.

When the day arrived, small and large yachts filled coves in the bay while the boating crowds jockeyed for position in the surrounding ocean at the starting point. All of the spectators who stood on the sands of Highland Beach were witnesses to history in the fall of 1899. The site overlooked the racecourse prepared for a best-of-five series. Accounts of the race reported that thousands of people lined the beaches between Sandy Hook and Long Branch to watch the yachts in action.

The plan to report the America's Cup races by Guglielmo Marconi's wireless transmission made exciting headlines. Stations were established at Sandy Hook and elsewhere along the course. The stations were laid out for transmitting messages recording the progress of the races to a point on the Irish coast in the neighborhood of Waterville. Preparations to make communication history appeared on the historic hills of Twin Lights near the north tower. The nearest crowds were electrified by the buzzing of the wireless spark gap transmitter. Reports from the *Grande Duchesse*, at sea among the competitors, were instantly wired to reporters at the *New York Herald*. Chris Brenner, in his documentary about Highland Beach, describes the event:

> *The America's Cup event was a very popular sporting event in this period, but difficult to watch from shore. News coverage became critical, and all*

the big New York papers would send reporters out on ships to capture the action. In 1899, Guglielmo Marconi set up a Morse code transmission site at Twin Lights, and put another transmitter on a ship near the race course. As race results came in, the news was transmitted back to Marconi at Twin Lights, where it then was passed by wire line to New York. The New York Herald, which sponsored the experiment, received over 2,000 words of news and went to press instantly, scooping all the other New York papers by a day. This was the first commercial application of radio transmission, and it changed the world forever.[40]

The calm waters in the coves of the Shrewsbury River at the southern end of Sandy Hook protected the racing yachts at night. The American sloop, *Columbia*, slid into the water after being outfitted in Bristol, Rhode Island, to defend the 1899 America's Cup. It had been anchored at Horseshoe Cove in the lower bay of Sandy Hook. Two dollars in your pocket bought you an early-morning ticket on the steamboat *Albertina*, carrying its passengers to the race of the century. Boats and steamers circled the racers while repeated cheers from onlookers encouraged the sailors waving their hats to the crowds while awaiting the signal. Thousands watched on the shore and viewed the scene from yachts anchored near the yard. The crowd of five thousand to six thousand cheering spectators at the starting point roared between the gun salutes and steam whistles in the harbor. The *Albertina* shadowed the sloops along the racecourse throughout the match. John King noted:

Barr successfully helmed the Columbia to victory, and Lipton's noted fair play provided unprecedented popular appeal to the sport and to his tea brand. An especially exciting race from the view point of the Irish Americans, or rather, a series of races, for the Cup was the challenge of Sir Thomas Lipton's Shamrock I representing Northern Ireland in 1899, the year Marconi's new wireless telegraph reported the minute by minute results. Lipton lost then, and again in 1901, 1903, 1920, and 1930, but good-naturedly, it was always said. The Highlands native, Edna McGuire Kruse, used to talk of Lipton stopping his boat at the Highlands and coming into the old McGuire house—after 1917, Bahrs Landing restaurant—or later on to the Kruse Pavilion for a quick glass of refreshment (not a tea!). She remembered him as a tall man, with a tanned face, steel gray hair, and a pleasure to talk to, a laugh-easy gentleman with a sly smile, honestly kind.[41]

There were three previous consecutive challenges, in 1885, 1886 and 1887, the only time in the history of this event that this has occurred three years in a row. The site continued to be popular for this famous yacht race. All six of the America's Cup races from 1893 through 1920 were held in the waters off Sandy Hook, easily within sight of most places in the Highlands and Highland Beach. They were the most exciting sporting events ever witnessed in American waters. Gambling was a big attraction, aided by up-to-the-minute race positions telegraphed by Marconi. Thomas Edison was quoted after learning of the success of Marconi's first transatlantic transmission at the Twin lighthouses in the hills of Navesink: "I would like to meet that young man who had the monumental audacity to attempt and succeed in jumping an electrical wave across the Atlantic."[42]

In 1905, the transatlantic race for the Kaiser's Cup presented a large fleet of sailing ships in the ocean and nearby Horseshoe Cove surrounding Sandy Hook. Eleven yachts were contending for the prize to cross the Atlantic, with a start point at Sandy Hook. A flotilla of private yachts worthy of the America's Cup event, with pennants flying, gathered nearby. Eleven yachts were entered in the race representing the United States, England and Germany. The Kaiser's Cup race was the fourth time sailing yachts had made the trip across the Atlantic up to that time. On the sands surrounding Highland Beach, they awaited the firing of the start gun at two o'clock in the afternoon. A final red ball would drop at 2:15 p.m. to start the ships on their three-thousand-mile journey, as told by the *New York Times* on May 16, 1905.[43]

15

MOVIES AT THE BEACH

By 1906, a new form of entertainment was sweeping the nation: the movies! Attracted by the popularity and excitement of the area, movie companies soon discovered this scenic location. This undeveloped rural area had much to offer in re-creating the feel of a desolate tropical island on the sands of Highland Beach. After filming the Spanish battleship *Viscaya* off the coast of Sandy Hook in February 1898, the American Mutoscope Company and Biograph Company of D.W. Griffith returned. The famous motion picture director brought the Biograph Company and actors to Highlands and nearby ocean beaches to shoot four films between 1908 and 1910. The films featured stars of great renown, including Mack Sennet, Linda Arvidson (later to become Mrs. Griffith) and Mary Pickford. A brief notice appeared in the *Red Bank Register* of July 20, 1910: "The American Biograph Company consisting of 40 persons were at the Martin House last week. The company is using the scenery at Highland Beach and surroundings for the production of moving pictures of seashore life."[44]

Historian John King pointed out in his article "Making Movies in Highlands" that people were already enthralled when they witnessed the silent films on screens across the town. The film crew suffered at their hands:

> *Griffith and his cameraman Bitzer were in town to shoot "A Salutary Life" and while doing it were tempted to shoot (with a gun) the unruly crowds gawking at the exciting happenings. Linda Arvidson in her autobiography, When the Movies were Young, tells about the incident. Before the summer*

> *was over we went to...Highlands. It wasn't very pleasant for here we encountered the summer boarder. As they had nothing better to do, they would see what we were going to do. We were generally being lovers, of course, and strolling in pairs beneath a sunshade until we reached the foreground, where we were to make a graceful flop onto the sandy beach and play our parts beneath the flirtatious parasol. Before we were ready to take the scene, we had to put up ropes to keep back the uninvited audience which giggled and tee-heed and commented loudly throughout. We felt like monkeys in a zoo, as if we'd gone back to the day when the populace jeered the old strolling players of Stratford town. Mr. Griffith got badly annoyed when we had such experiences....One saving grace the Highlands had for us. We could get a swim sometimes.*[45]

Initially, the first Highlands moving picture venues were not theaters at all. Stores and open lots were quickly set up to project the movies for the folks in town reacting to the fad. Johnson's Miller Street drugstore had an adjoining store outfitted for the movie fans, attracting a full house. A park and indoor sites showing movies in Highlands were well patronized. Often, the show comprised a vaudeville performance, motion pictures and hit songs. Watching movies under the stars in the open air had its advantages on warm nights.

A couple at Highland Beach playing a movie part beneath the flirtatious parasol, circa 1910. *Courtesy of the Historical Society of Highlands archive.*

Will Sandlass searched for different types of entertainment to meet the expectations of his visitors. Having a seat on Highland Beach to watch the movie-making business inspired Sandlass. He was ready to incorporate movie viewing into the resort experience. One such idea took Will and Catherine to the Caribbean islands in search of bamboo to build an outdoor theater at Highland Beach. Adapting to the new lifestyle came easy to his family, as they enjoyed the winter trips south to investigate greater and more exciting amusements to bring back to the resort at Highland Beach. The racehorse circuit from Saratoga Springs to Cuba was a fascination for Will and his brother Louis through the years. In 1908, he, Catherine and Louis took a trip to Cuba in search of a tropical spirit to enhance the resort. His idea to reproduce the island flavors in the northern climates took hold of his imagination. When the ship left port in Cuba and headed to its destination in Jamaica before returning to the States, Will had all he needed to match the dream. The ship's hold was filled to the brim with bamboo, palm trees and furniture to emulate all he had seen on the voyage. The trip home was a difficult one for Catherine. She suffered terrible bouts of seasickness all the way home. When Will, Catherine and Louis reached New York Harbor in June, she was immediately transported to a local hospital for treatment. No one realized the severity of her illness. Within two weeks, Will had lost his wife to the sickness, and his son, Bill, had lost his mother. His brother, Louis, was still grieving from the loss of his wife, Jennie, years before in Baltimore. The success of the business was a distraction rather than a consolation for the family. In spite of his loss, Will continued with his plans to convert the resort into new venues for summer visitors in the early twentieth century.

A train pulled up to the New Jersey mill in Long Branch with its cargo of bamboo. Carload after carload was emptied as the greatly anticipated bamboo for the new rustic garden was delivered to the mill of the Edwards Lumber & Coal Company in Long Branch. The green bamboo from Cuba was twelve feet long and three to five inches in diameter. The workmen unloaded fifty thousand lineal feet of bamboo. The intended space at Highland Beach was eighty feet square, with the expectation that the attraction would be without parallel on the Jersey coast. The plans moved forward to open the palm gardens in June 1908.

The first Merry-Go-Round was moved, and the interior space became the Bamboo Garden. An airdrome was built in the shape of a fort with the ubiquitous pennants flying. The palm tree was so large that part of the roof had to be removed to accommodate its height in the new Bamboo Garden. Will Sandlass opened the "Airdrome Theatre"—an open-air movie venue converted from an outdoor deck on the river side. In the early 1900s, the public's love for movies could be enjoyed under the stars in the Airdrome, featuring the Triangle Players from the Triangle Motion Picture Company and filmmaker, D.W. Griffith. Visitors could also listen to ragtime in the cabaret. The Bamboo Bar was brother Johnson's domain, located on the ground floor of the Billiards and Bowling building and opened to the public within the year. The Highland Beach entertainment hot spot made the news far into the ragtime era. The resort grew through the first decade of the twentieth century, when steamboats, trains and automobiles brought more

People gather at the Highland Beach Airdrome and Bamboo Garden to watch the latest films under the stars featuring the Triangle Studio Players movie company. *Author's collection.*

people to the shore and to the new Bamboo Garden cabaret, an outdoor dance hall on the river side of the resort. Documentarian Chris Brenner explained the experience in retrospect:

> *During the winters in this period, Sandlass liked to travel to Florida and Cuba, and took a liking to the look of bamboo and palm trees. He arranged for the shipments of the material to be sent to Highland Beach, and that décor graced the new theater and even more of the resort later on. But screening wasn't the only connection to the movie industry—famous director D.W. Griffith filmed four movies between 1908 and 1910 on the beach at the site. Visitors could watch the filming from the boardwalk, adding yet another draw, and making Highland Beach famous in movie houses across the country.*[46]

16

RESORT GROWTH BOOMS

From the 1890s until 1910, there was a progressive growth in Highlands' population when the summer populace peaked in this vacationer's paradise. Gambling, horse racing and parlor games were popular until 1894, when anti-gambling forces were successful in effecting a statewide ban. Horse racing and legal parlor games could no longer be enjoyed throughout the state of New Jersey. After 1900, Asbury Park rivaled Long Branch and Atlantic City as the most popular resort. New transportation modes enhanced the success of Highland Beach.

Between 1900 and 1906, Will Sandlass expanded his business interests at the shore and invested further in the Highland Beach resort and applied cost-saving measures. The contents of the Cheeseborough Building Saloon and its liquor license on State Street in Manhattan were offered for sale. Will took advantage of the opportunity to make the purchase. At the resort, he completed an artificial pond filled with water using the water main to provide his own ice for the resort's icehouse rather than paying a local company to deliver it. The pond provided several tons of six-inch-thick, first-class ice in winter. When summer arrived, the pond was stocked with water lilies and two fountains to please the arriving guests exiting from the nearby trains.

October to May each year offered opportunities for new ventures. The Sandlass construction company had contracts in the off-season. The Gideon Stock Farm hired him to build a new stable and jockey's quarters. Locals Henry Schenck and John N. Johnson were part of Will's construction crew that boarded at the site for three months. Another endeavor by Sandlass included T. Hettrick of New York and William Gelhaus of Atlantic Highlands. They organized a stock company to manufacture brick and other clay products in Cliffwood, New Jersey. The company was incorporated with a capital stock of $125,000 and a paid-up capital of $1,000,000. The brickyard had an annual capacity of ten million bricks. The new company modernized to increase output. An order for three million bricks was received following the incorporation.

Another gale-force storm struck in early May 1903. Two men were out for a day's fishing when the storm unexpectedly appeared near Scotland light on the coast of Sandy Hook. Unable to reach shore, the boat suddenly capsized opposite the Sandlass Pavilion. Some of the Sandlass women noticed the men struggling in the water. They alerted Johnson Sandlass and lifesaver John Mattingly, who jumped into a surf boat and went to the rescue. Both of the fishermen clung to the boat for survival. Unfortunately, one lost his grip and was carried out to sea. Johnson and John, with the aid of a rope and a pipe, were able to pull the other man to safety. The survivor remained at the Sandlass home until he recovered.

The year 1908 was a great one of transformation. The former Merry-Go-Round building underwent a metamorphosis, revealing the new Bamboo Garden. This place was a principal attraction of the resort, where patrons danced into the night listening to strains of violin, flute and piano music. Inside the Bamboo Garden, Japanese parasols adorned the space. In other areas around the resort, electric wiring updated and overhauled the buildings for basket parties and bathing-suit rentals. Renovations were completed in the Photographic Gallery, improvements were made to the beach platform and a new walk was laid down from the Bamboo Garden to the old pier of the Patten Line near the government reservation. Two social clubs appeared at Highland Beach during the same summer season: the Dar-He Club was converted from a building owned by the Highland Beach Improvement Company next to the Surf House hotel, and the Surf Club opened within the hotel. John King noted in his book *Highlands, New Jersey*: "The whole resort complex was in Ocean Township, that is, until the Borough of Sea Bright annexed it on March 31, 1909. Soon its owner, Will Sandlass, bringing with him over a quarter of a million dollars in ratables, won election as a town council member of the borough."[47] Will's future service as a council member increased his association with leaders in the community. Highland Beach became a center for political dinners hosted at the Surf House hotel.

Will was ready for the big crowds after his improvements over the winter. The parlor of the Surf House hotel, refitted with bamboo, was the place where ten-cent quatrefoil coins could be purchased for admission to dance at the Bamboo Garden. The rustic Bamboo Garden was designed for 2,500 people. It was enlarged and covered with a large pergola surrounding it. The ballroom and its large dance floor had a tropical atmosphere. It was adjoined by an open-air pavilion decorated with palms and coconut leaves. The pavilion was capable of seating one thousand people and for serving light meals and other refreshments with a view of the river. The big attraction in the Bamboo Garden was located overhead in a preserved coconut palm that soared toward the dome. George M. Foster of Highlands, who supervised the building of the Bamboo Garden, carefully replaced the preserved palm ferns on the tree. Stuffed monkeys and birds were set about the garden. Will's alligator, brought from Florida and mounted in New York, was residing high within the tree. Business was booming, and land values in Highlands had more than doubled over a few years.

The *Red Bank Register* of July 7, 1909, had a story describing the crowds at Highland Beach.

> *These crowds were greater than ever seen before when 15,000 people were at the Highlands and 10,000 at Highland Beach on Saturday and more on Sunday during the holiday weekend. Many people had to go back because they were unable to find accomodations. Ten thousand people were cared for by Sandlass over the weekend. Throngs of people arrived, all were served at the restaurant and those requesting bathing suits. No one was turned away. All venues were jammed constantly with people requesting pictures in the gallery or enjoying the bowling lanes. An enormous amount of soda was consumed at the counters and in the crowded fountain booths. Out on the river, 300–400 boats filled the river on Sunday to Monday.*[48]

According to news reports, it was difficult for a boat to make its way through the fleet.

In the early part of the twentieth century, the resort growth was building to a crescendo. Growth of shore communities was at its zenith and increasing. In 1910, the summer visitors increased again when more than twenty thousand tourists filled all liveable space on both land and sea in the town of Highlands over the Fourth of July, according to weekend reports. On Sunday alone, the record-breaking crowd applied for 3,000 bathing suits and the same on Monday at Highland Beach. The rented suits were washed in carbolic soap

The trolley on the other side of the bridge between Highlands and Highland Beach allowed visitors a short walk to the excursion resort. *Author's collection.*

and hung to dry on racks above the Bathing Pavilion, ready for another user. Occasionally, suits were thrown over the bathhouse lockers to an awaiting friend, saving the rental fee. The volume of summer mail caused the post office to open a new facility in the same year. Over ten thousand postal cards were mailed from the Highlands, in excess of any previous record in one weekend. In John King's article "Penny Post Cards Preserve the Past," he reminds us of Will Sandlass's entrepreneurial spirit. He saw a golden opportunity to promote his Sandlass Pavilion through producing "Souvenir Postal Cards" and join the fad in the early years of the twentieth century to increase the visibility of his resort: "He publicized his resort across the river on Sandy Hook with more than two-dozen self-published scenes of people cavorting in the river or ocean waters.…Usually local photographers like Foxwell took the photographs for the private publishers such as Johnson (Highlands Pharmacy) and Sandlass. These were sent to Dresden, Germany, for color lithographic printing with about a year turn-around time from initial photograph to actual display and sales."[49]

These images captured the attention of the day tripper making plans for a sojourn to the shore. Receiving the "Wish you were here!" cards piqued more interest in popular destinations, and this personal advertising sparked a longing for more time at the beach. Lazy days among the houseboats,

Bathers cavorting in the river, Highland Beach, New Jersey. William Sandlass's postcards were available to advertise the resort in Highlands and Highland Beach, 1905. *Author's collection.*

tents and bungalows afforded a perfect playground for anyone wishing to get away from the heat and hectic pace. Power yachts and canoes cruised the shores by the scrub marshes filled with nature's wildlife, providing ample room to make this one of the most popular resorts of its day. According to contemporary reports, it was hard to find a rendezvous with more houseboats moored in one harbor in the late 1880s than the one between Highlands and Highland Beach.

A wooden walkway nearby led to a seventy-five-foot steamboat dock on the Shrewsbury River where incoming passengers could easily disembark for a short walk to the attractions at Highland Beach. At the far end of the Sandlass property, closer to the military reservation on Sandy Hook, twenty-five summer bungalows grew over time, beginning with one houseboat owner's request to winter onshore. The colony continued to evolve spontaneously following the response to the man who asked Sandlass if he could put his houseboat on the property that winter. Will Sandlass saw an opportunity to lease the land. Soon, many others came to request space next to the bathhouses at the north end of the excursion resort. As the requests started to increase, a new business developed when Will agreed to lease the lots. Each occupant who was willing to erect a summer cottage could rent space to build their summer home. The bungalows were filled with generations of families who returned each summer for decades to come.

Before 1910, there wasn't an official designation to signify the government lands at the southern end of the Sandy Hook peninsula. When a boundary monument was built at the north end of the resort near the military reservation, it eliminated any confusion about where the military property began and Highland Beach resort ended. No more sightseers or excursionists would be allowed to cross this line without a pass. Inside the Fort Hancock grounds, the base canteen that served beer to soldiers and guests had closed down. Once the canteen was no longer available, the soldiers joined in the entertainments at the nearby resort on Saturday nights. The change from beer to a variety of alcoholic beverages caused overindulgence, according to the superior officers at Fort Hancock. It was a bone of contention with the military base's top-ranking officers when the soldiers returned to the barracks. Eventually, the soldiers were restricted from going to the Highland Beach bars. This was no doubt a relief for both sides of the dilemma.

Winter brought time for renewal when Will, his mother and the family traveled to Florida, where he managed a hotel and clubhouse near Tampa during the winter season in 1910. While in Florida, storms took their toll on the resort buildings and cottages in the off-season. The storms of the winter played havoc with the boardwalk. The Highland Beach boardwalk, an attraction for hundreds of people, was almost completely demolished. Part of it was carried out to sea; the rest of it lay strewn all

Christy family enjoying summer life in the Bungalow Colony at Highland Beach, some of the earliest residents on Dock Street. *Courtesy of the Jill Walters collection.*

over the railroad tracks and boulders on the seawall. Will returned to put his enterprises in good condition to open the season. His mother, Annie, had been ill, although she recovered in time to return to her Fruit Stand, which had moved to the Surf House after the Bamboo Bar took its place in the Bowling and Billiards building.

The night watchman at Highland Beach played a significant part in keeping the premises safe from intruders in the late-evening and early-morning hours. James Hyers of Belford was one of the first to be hired as a security guard after he was injured in an accident at Sandy Hook. Despite losing an arm, he continued to work at the Sandlass Pavilion for several years and tended his flower and vegetable garden in Belford. Howard Johnson followed in Hyers's footsteps in the summer of 1911. Referred to as "burly," his stature was considered enough to deter anyone from breaking the law. A highly anticipated season opened with the first dance held in the Bamboo Garden on a Saturday night. Dancing continued until nearly midnight to the music of the same orchestra of the last three years. A large number of boxwoods had been placed in pots in the open-air pavilion, adding to the attractive air about the dance floor. The popular Sunday afternoon and evening concerts were featured again. The Dar-He and Surf Clubs opened their clubhouses adjacent to the west side of Surf Avenue between the depot and the Sandlass property. Both clubs had chefs, and members spent many hours there during the summer. The chef held his annual cakewalk and dance at the Dar-He Club. The cakewalk tradition, dating from the Civil War, was originally performed by slaves on plantation grounds with a cake as the prize. This form of dance eventually became a popular feature of minstrel shows, and local cakewalk championships were hosted in New York's Madison Square Garden. Cakewalk dances eventually gave rise to their own form of music, an early predecessor of ragtime. The Surf House hosted the 1912 annual cakewalk for the staff of the Creighton and Thompson Hotels in Highlands and Navesink, Sea Bright and Asbury Park. Several awards were made by the judges from New York to the black performers for the best cakewalking. About five hundred were present at the event, where dancing was enjoyed until 2:00 a.m. Later in the evening, the resort hosted a dance for the performers to enjoy their own music. Crowds at Highlands and Highland Beach were the largest in the history of the place.

17

TECHNOLOGY AND TRANSPORTATION CHANGES

The auto age came to Atlantic City just before the twentieth century began, when an imported French electric car appeared on its streets. This changed life at the shore more than the arrival of the railroads, marking the beginning of a new era. The electric car was the forerunner of automobiles and their impact, which would change life at the beach. Highland Beach faced the challenge of limited parking to keep pace with the influx of visitors in their new motorcars. The stable was converted to a social club due to the lack of requests for livery. Harold Wilson in his book *The Story of the Jersey Shore* writes about the automobile's coming invasion: "By 1900 the age of the automobile was at hand In fact, until the democratization of the automobile in the 1920's, the horse continued to figure importantly in the lives of most shore people. A study of census figures indicates that the number of horses mounted steadily in the four shore counties throughout the nineteenth century. The number of horses reached its peak in 1910, as automobiles and trucks began to increase."[50]

"Diamond" Jim Brady, a financier known for his lavishness, had six electric cars at his disposal while living in Long Branch at the beginning of the twentieth century. At first, curiosity brought out onlookers, wondering how the cars worked. These novelties, originally available only for the most fashionable, became an alternative way of getting to the shore. Observing the new advantages of automobiles to bring in the crowds, shore towns hosted races on the beach. Better automobile roads and bridges became a priority with local media and state legislators. Taxes on New Jersey residents for road maintenance soon caused controversy in the days of early car regulation. The completion of Fort Hancock impacted access to land adjoining Highland Beach, serving the crowds crossing over the boundary line.

By 1903, the stockholders of the Seabright and Highlands Turnpike had offered to sell the road to the county for $4,000. A dispute erupted over the cost of the road, and citizens of Sea Bright signaled willingness to contribute the difference in the sale price in order to avoid the annoyance of paying tolls. Additional boathouse landings were in operation at Highland Beach in 1907. The two steamboat piers awaited passengers on the Shrewsbury River during the summer season. One pier was strategically placed in a diagonal manner near the walking bridge deep into the river. The second pier operated at the end of the expanding Bungalow Colony on Dock Street where the Mel-Rah Club (former stable) existed close to the entrance of Fort Hancock. Both small and larger steamboats had a place to come. The deeper waters needed for the larger boats, beyond the sandbar on Dock Street, afforded enough depth for the necessary docking of a 175-foot-long vessel. This dock placement allowed for the steamboat to be far enough away from the bridge to make the run across the river to Highlands safely at the Schenk's ferry landing and other docks nearby.

The Central Railroad of New Jersey train coming through the Highlands Bridge to Highland Beach excursion resort, seen in a postcard sent to Uncle Fritz. *Author's collection, 1912.*

Above: The Horton's Ice Cream specialty sign advertised prominently in front of the Candy Store opposite the rail station at Highland Beach. *Author's collection.*

Left: Entrance to the Bamboo Garden interior under the rustic dome at Highland Beach on a summer day awaiting the arrival of its first visitors. *Author's collection.*

The forty-fifth anniversary and final year of the Highlands Ferry was celebrated in November 1910. James Schenck's ferry service had opened up travel to the peninsula. He transported passengers and cargo across the Shrewsbury River to make a connection with the railroad on Sandy Hook. At first, he used a "rowed" ferry and later a steam ferry to handle the large number of visitors from New York by rail. Two years later, the Central Railroad made a much-needed change to the Highlands drawbridge and trestle leading to the resort. The railroad built a footbridge on the north side of the draw from the station platform, giving pedestrians all the room possible. The wagon bridge was placed on the south side so as not to endanger the lives of hundreds of people who in the summer crossed the bridge every day.

Visitors continued to arrive on trains screeching to a halt on scorching hot days. Passengers ignored the push of the crowds bursting forth into the sunshine for a glimpse of the place. A cacophony of sounds swirled around them in the heat: engine whistles, steamboat horns and the chatter of tourists disembarking. Squeals of laughter came from all directions.

For those arrivals parched with thirst, the famous New York City Horton's Ice Cream sign and the Highland Beach ice cream/candy store with thirst-quenching cola was just across the path. Another train pulled into the station as Highland Beach opened its arms to the flood of visitors!

PART V

War, Economics and Social Changes

1912–1940

After the war, good times returned as the nation entered the roaring 20's. The Monmouth County area took hold as THE place to summer. Jazz music was in fashion, and Highland Beach responded by hiring popular bands to play in the Bamboo Garden on weekends.…Of course, with the start of Prohibition, Highland Beach was dealt a blow—the revenue stream from alcohol sales stopped, and things started to change. Much of the New York tourist trade slowed, but more local, permanent residents remained as the area gentrified.

—Chris Brenner

The St. Lawrence River canoe was one of the popular features at Highland Beach. Rented bathing suits hung from drying poles above bathhouses. *Author's collection.*

18

A NEW LIFE

Music and contemporary diversions played an important part in the evolution of Highland Beach through the decades as a source of entertainment and social gathering. Values of the period rooted in religion, morality and an industrial work ethic were in flux as the new era brought a more relaxed code of conduct and an emphasis on implementation of standard inventions used in the modern world. The resort thrived as the middle class enjoyed leisure-time activities. The 1911 summer season opened with entirely renovated bathhouses and extra pavilions to meet the needs of the increasing number of excursionists. The *Red Bank Register* reported on July 31, 1912: "The proprietor of the Highlands photo studio, near the bamboo garden at Highland Beach, has built a miniature aeroplane in the rear of the studio. Persons get into the aeroplane by ladder and when sitting for a picture they appear as if soaring through the air. The pictures are reproduced on post cards and they are one of the leading souvenirs this summer of Highland Beach. The pictures show the Twin lighthouses in the background."[51]

Andrew Coleman had replaced Mr. Vantine in the photography studio. When out on a photo shoot one day, Coleman was getting his camera ready to take a picture on private property. To his surprise, the overzealous local police nabbed him for trespassing on property, not realizing he had permission to be on the grounds. Coleman told the judge he preferred a little less zeal on the part of the police.

Above: Earl Fuller's Famous Jazz Band (1918) performed at Rector's in New York City and at the Highland Beach Bamboo Garden, featuring Ted Lewis and Teddy Brown. *Unknown photographer. Courtesy of www.wvxu.org.*

Opposite: Portrait of William Sandlass, proprietor of Highland Beach excursion resort, New Jersey, circa 1912. *Author's collection.*

Flags fluttered in August 1912 at the Bamboo Garden during the most anticipated event of the season. A Masquerade Ball filled the pavilion with four hundred guests. Many traveled from New York to compete for prizes awarded to guests with the most original costumes. A dress covered in newspaper clippings, a gypsy, a sailor and Buster Brown were favorites. The most enchanting moment of the evening occurred when Johnson Sandlass danced the waltz with his mother, Annie, who never missed a good dance at the Garden. Refreshments arrived at midnight, and the dancing continued far into the night under the stars.

An unexpected change came into Will's life at the age of forty-eight. His friends brought new possibilities into his world. As business prospered, Will's close friend Henry Schaad, a treasurer at the Belasco Theatre in New York, cajoled the widower into going to the city on a regular basis. The Hotel Gerard, next door to the Belasco, was a convenient place to stay and make telephone calls to his son Bill about the resort happenings. On one of his visits, Will encountered Helen and Mae Lynch at the hotel's telephone exchange.

Helen and Mae, first-generation Irish, lived in the Kips Bay neighborhood with their family members—father Michael, mother Bridget and sister Katie—on the far east side of Manhattan on Forty-First Street and First Avenue. As many Irish immigrants did when they arrived, Michael found work as a waiter, at the Hotel Gerard on West Forty-Fourth Street. This led to an opportunity for his daughters to join the hotel staff. Being next to a theater, Helen was selected as the role model for the actress playing a telephone girl. She was chosen by theater owner David Belasco when he staged *The Woman*. Seated at the telephone switchboard in the Hotel Gerard, her fate changed when Will Sandlass appeared. According to contemporary accounts, her friend Phoebe Levine had foretold Helen's future. Phoebe forecasted that she would meet a tall man with good fortune. Helen believed her, and the following week, a tall man appeared at the hotel. His diamond scarfpin caught the light as he paid for the telephone call. He returned several times to make more calls. He remarked on the pleasant weather and wished she could enjoy some of it. Without embarrassment, he asked, "Would you care to dine with me tonight, Miss Lynch?" Helen kept him waiting even after learning that Will Sandlass owned a hotel at Highland Beach. He was persistent. At last, one evening, she accepted his invitation to dine. Will hailed a carriage to return her home in style. As they arrived at the front door, her father stepped out. Michael Lynch, not pleased at the site of a fancy carriage in a working-class neighborhood, approached with a threatening glare to warn Helen's suitor of the impression he gave. Nevertheless, the courtship began. A few days after meeting, Will finalized a real estate deal that brought him a profit. He considered Helen his good-luck charm and named her his "Lucky Billikin." Their two-year romance captured the attention of journalists because of Will's well-recognized name in the business community. The engagement story was published up and down the East Coast. A *Miami Herald* news release hailed the meeting of Helen and William as "a love story in a sweet tale." Helen told the paper's news reporter the story while packing her trunk. She confessed that the twenty-five-year age difference was nothing when there was love. Will's gallant and gentlemanly display of affection with gifts, dinners and plays endeared him to her. After they became officially engaged, she immediately left the Gerard Hotel to rush around and plan the wedding. She gave him the Irish name *Billo* and, as a wedding gift, presented Will with a gold Billikin lucky piece to show she appreciated the nickname he had given her.[52]

He married his pretty little Irish girl in the rectory of St. Agnes Catholic Church at 7:30 p.m. on a September evening in 1912. The dark-haired fortune-teller Phoebe Levine was bridesmaid, and Henry Schaad was best man. As the sun set in the Manhattan sky, a supper awaited them nearby at the elegant restaurant Louis Martin's on Broadway between Forty-First and Forty-Second Streets, a popular spot with the theater crowds. The two-month honeymoon plans included a Baltimore visit to introduce Helen to the family, a trip to the Pamunkey River Indian Reservation near Will's Virginia hunting lodge and a winter stay in Palm Beach.

On Will's return to Highland Beach with his new bride, they received good wishes at a special dinner. His fellow town council members and Mayor George Elliott presented Will with a silver loving cup inscribed, "Presented to Hon. William Sandlass by the Mayor and Council of the Borough of Sea Bright, November 21, 1912." The kind feelings of his colleagues touched Will, according to reports. Helen and Will returned from their honeymoon with tales of a southern sojourn to Palm Beach and a steamboat trip to New Orleans, where Helen learned to make a southern specialty from the riverboat's chef. The chef's distinctive style of cooking seared the Canadian bacon. He then put it into a cream sauce sizzling with flavor in a hot iron skillet. The fancy dish became a favorite at the resort. Helen had time on her hands during the boat trip, while Will tried his luck at cards. It was a foreshadowing of luck and loss in the years ahead.

Sister Mae had married a young Frank Smith from their Manhattan neighborhood a year earlier, in 1911. Mae and Frank joined Will and Helen at Highland Beach each summer, arriving with their growing family of red-headed children. Mae would be an important part of the staff, and Helen would go on to become a very active member of the Highland Beach management. Helen operated the Bathing Pavilion and other attractions, while Mae managed the Novelty Store near the bridge. Helen and Mae's mother, Bridget Lynch, joined the family and enlarged workforce at the resort along with Will's mother, Annie, at the Fruit & Cigar Stand each summer. Helen was due to give birth to their first child in December 1913. As winter arrived and the due date for the baby grew closer, a horrific winter storm approached the coast on December 26, 1913.

A three-day blizzard raged on Sandy Hook, resulting in a storm of the century. On December 28, 1913, Henry Sandlass was born in the midst of a winter hurricane that prevented the doctor from reaching the Sandy Hook peninsula to assist Helen. The baby was named after Will's closest friend, Henry Schaad, who had passed away from an illness the previous August. Sea Bright was devastated after a second storm arrived a week later, on January 3–5, 1914. They were the worst storms in twenty-five

Sandlass's Bamboo Garden, winter, circa 1912. *Author's collection.*

years, with an estimated loss of over $500,000 (approximately $13,000,000 in 2019). The *Long Branch Daily Record* reported at the time: "Going down the almost impassable country road toward the Highland bridge, the ocean boulevard prevents an inviting appearance. The Sandlass boardwalk at Highland Beach was washed away. The bulkhead was also more or less damaged. All during the night the residents of Sea Bright worked hard to relieve the suffering and inconvenience of the families who were deprived of their homes....It was the worst calamity that has been experienced in the little city [Sea Bright] located between river and ocean since the fire holocaust of twenty-two years ago."[53]

Henry was to be the only child of Helen and Will, due to complications during his birth. Henry's christening at Our Lady of Perpetual Help in Highlands brought together the couple's close friends to celebrate this momentous occasion for the Sandlass family. Mayor Elliott and Mike Jacobs, the famous boxing promoter of New York City, joined the family party at the Sandlass home after the ceremony. As soon as spring arrived, the storm restorations began.

Will's business interests extended beyond the resort. His entrepreneurship even extended to selling tickets for shows, ferries and sporting events in tandem with other partners who had ties to New York City and the shore resort. The Bungalow Colony expanded again when two Sandlass bungalows were added

Helen Sandlass and son Henry sitting at the Highland Beach excursion resort near a rustic fence on a summer day, 1913. *Author's collection.*

to the property. On the busiest weekends at the beach, Will continued to hire extra staff to man the restaurants and music venues at Highland Beach. Earl Fuller's ragtime band came from Rector's Restaurant in New York City as a featured act for the Police Ball. A cabaret performance with New York actresses entertained every Saturday night. In August, Rector's Tango Band played for the Annual Board of Trade Dinner Dance at the Bamboo Garden where the secretary of war, L.M. Garrison, attended the annual banquet. First-class vaudeville, moving pictures and cabaret shows gave audiences an expanded selection of diversions each day. Highland Beach was full to overflowing with guests. Staff and family members manned their posts in locations throughout the resort, including the hotel, novelty and ice cream store, Bathing Pavilion offices, Bamboo Garden Pavilion and Bamboo Bar. After a six-year absence, because of the original Merry-Go-Round removal to make space for the Bamboo Garden, the guests at the resort once again enjoyed a ride on the carousel under a domed roof in its new location near the bridge. At the beginning of the 1914 season, the bowling alleys were also converted into a dance hall decorated with freshly painted red walls and ornamental lights. Frank Smith, his brother-in-law, had experience handling cash for the American Express Company in Manhattan, a forerunner of today's Amex. He calculated the earnings to go to the bank on Monday mornings and was entrusted with the deposit for the resort revenue each week. Each family member at the resort had a part in the success of the burgeoning business, building at a faster rate than ever anticipated.

The shared space on Sandy Hook between the resort and the fort called for increasing awareness of the limits set by the military. In spite of the U.S. reservation boundaries, fishermen continued to fish north of Highland Beach even though bathers were not allowed to swim in the waters at this location. Success continued even though transportation to the resort was in the process of change. It came gradually at first. The number of steamboats on the Shrewsbury River started to decrease. According to Jean Howson, in *An Illustrated History of Travel & Transportation*, there were only five smaller steam vessels running in 1915 on the river. The Central Railroad's famed "Sandy Hook Route" carried the largest numbers of passengers to Atlantic Highlands on its two huge steamers, the *Monmouth* and the *Sandy Hook*. They then caught a train on the short rail connection to the resort.[54] The Bamboo Garden still advertised the Highlands trolley connection for evening dances throughout the summer season.

Will Sandlass's family helped operate the business as his children reached adulthood. His oldest son, Bill, from his first marriage, branched out in 1915

The Sandlass Bros. Bathing Pavilion, Sea Bright, New Jersey, circa 1923. The bathing pavilion is known today as Chapel Beach Club. *Courtesy of the Robert Schoeffling collection.*

when he leased the bathing establishment from the owners, Shropshire & Elliott, in the heart of Sea Bright's town center. The Sandlass Bros. sign displayed over the entrance recognized his silent partner (younger brother Henry). Within a few years, the Presbyterian Chapel was annexed to the Sandlass Bros. Bathing Pavilion when the business was stretched beyond its capacity. In order to take care of the increased popularity, the house of worship was converted into a bathing structure. (The flagpole in the accompanying photo is shown at half-mast due to the passing of President Warren Harding on August 2, 1923.)

Each new summer was subject to unexpected change. The year 1916 brought the trauma of shark attacks along the northern Jersey coast. Chris Brenner's Highland Beach documentary highlighted a summer of fear at the Jersey Shore:

> *The news in the summer of 1916 featured a startling turn of events at the Jersey Shore that shocked the nation and actually created a local business that is still a favorite today.*
>
> *That summer, what is thought to be a Great White shark made its way from Long Beach Island, all the way to Matawan Creek, attacking five people and killing four of them along the way, including children swimming far inland in the creek. The effect on tourism was devastating, with many beach closings, and others placing nets around swimming areas in an effort to make swimmers feel comfortable.*
>
> *In Highlands, a local boat rental business at the foot of Miller St., saw its customers all but disappear. No one wanted to be in the water in small boats fishing and crabbing. The Bahr's family needed to make ends meet, so they purchased a building near the foot of the bridge across from Highland Beach and started to sell food to tourists. Bahr's restaurant became a local and regional favorite, still run by the same family nearly 100 years later.*[55]

Shark attacks ceased that summer without agreement as to whether this was the same shark or not. Bathers were harder to convince that the threat was gone. It was reported in the *Red Bank Register* on August 9, 1916: "The shark scare at Highland Beach has quieted down, much to the satisfaction of the bathers. On Sunday, the beach was thronged with bathers and a large number of persons had to be turned away for lack of bathhouses."[56]

The extra measure of a steel lifeboat was secured to improve bathing safety at Highland Beach. In addition, an expansion was made to one of

Bahrs, a still popular seafood restaurant today, is located next to the Highlands, New Jersey bridge. The vintage photo is circa 1940s. *Courtesy of Cosgrove/Bahrs collection.*

the most unique gardens along the seashore, the Bamboo Garden. It was designed after the roof garden of the Hotel Astor in New York. Instead of being painted, it had an original appearance called a "green pea effect" surrounded by potted shrubbery and cultivated flowers accentuated by colored lights on the veranda. The pergola with twelve columns made of white ash, transported from Virginia, surrounded the garden built to withstand the winter winds. The outdoor patio and Airdrome to view moving pictures was attached to the Bamboo Garden.

John Mulhern, a local teenager, worked at Sandlass's soda fountain during the years he grew up on Sandy Hook. He reminisced in a 1984 interview with Tom Hoffman, the National Park Service historian at Sandy Hook, about his time at the Pavilion in the early 1900s:

> *Every Saturday night, the place would be bouncing at the seams. Tom Garrity was working in the Bamboo Garden putting on the cabaret shows, principally singing. He was a character from New York City associated with "Rector's Famous Band." Saturday night, I worked in the ice cream store until 1 o'clock in the morning. There was the Sandlass candy store where they sold Horton's ice cream. An express wagon delivered the ice cream from Horton's Ice Cream Company of Fulton Street in Brooklyn.*

The Bamboo Garden Airdrome, with pictures and dancing, combined in one admission with movies shown by starlight, circa 1917. *Author's collection.*

They sold Hire's Root Beer and Moxy in a tin can. Moxy is something like Coca-Cola, a little more bitter. There was a sign over the ice cream parlor with a finger pointing one way. Moxy for you! No matter where you walked, the eyes and fingers always followed you. It was ten cents for a small drink. A Hershey bar was a nickel and ice cream sundaes cost twenty cents.

At the restaurant [Basket Pavilion], *you have a thousand people dropped in your lap at 11 o'clock in the morning after they have just had an hour and a half ride on a train. They are all hungry and thirsty and they dash to this Pavilion. They had about three or four waiters there all the time…when Sandlass knew there were two excursions coming in, that meant 2,200 people, he would need more waiters. So, evidently, there was a hiring hall or something in New York because he had a contact with this place. He would say, "Send me 10 waiters." And they had a place for these guys to sleep overnight at Sandlass Beach. In the Sandlass Hotel* [Surf House], *they had a real nice*

> *restaurant with white tablecloths in the building across the street from the ice cream store. The waiters had a white coat, a short formal jacket. Every once in a while, they would have quite a display of flags and it was really a very colorful sort of thing.*[57]

Following the outbreak of World War I in 1914, the population was distracted. The summer season ended, and more pressing news filled the papers as the months unfolded.

19

WORLD WAR I IMPACT

The Jersey Shore sunseekers had faced dangers from fires and storms in previous years. World War I threatened the United States when it joined the war in April 1917. Although the general population felt protected by an ocean from the menace abroad, they did not account for the changes in technology and communications over the decades that made them vulnerable on the Atlantic coast. German U-boats began to stalk the coast of Sandy Hook, creating fear. Americans were asleep to the threat before the lights-out drills practiced onshore. Communities were increasingly faced with dangers lurking in the waters off the coastline. Of the 360 U-boats deployed by Germany during the war, 6 were sent across the Atlantic to threaten shipping from Virginia to New York. During the war, German U-boats along the East Coast sank close to one hundred vessels and left more than four hundred people dead. A U-boat was bold enough to shell Fort Hancock one summer evening. At the north end of Sandy Hook, shots from the vessel landed near the Coast Guard station. Fortunately, no damage was done. The next year, eighteen French soldiers were stationed at Fort Hancock testing large field pieces. The recoil from the guns was so strong that it shook the earth for miles around. The nearby residents were kept busy trying to protect their porcelain and pictures from falling. The most important effect in Monmouth County was the establishment of a military base, Camp Alfred Vail, as a Signal Corps center on the old Monmouth Park grounds that would later become Fort Monmouth.

Smith family at Surf House hotel, Highland Beach, circa 1929. *Back row, left to right*: Frank, Rita, Mae and Doris. *Front row, left to right*: Marie and Fran. *Courtesy of the Frank Smith collection.*

During this time, young Henry Sandlass was a small child who had companionship only in the summers. His aunt and uncle, Mae Smith and her husband, Frank, continued to spend summers at the Highland Beach resort's Surf House hotel. Mae and Frank had their first child, Helen, just a month before cousin Henry was born. They would go on to have five additional children. As Henry became older, the off-seasons and winters were a lonely place for a child. The Smith children were surrogate sisters and brothers to Henry until it was time for them to return to the Bronx during the long off-season months. Since Henry had not yet reached school age, Helen talked with sister Mae about her worries for Henry's wintertime melancholy. At first, Mae sent her young daughter Helen to the resort to spend time and help with the loneliness felt by her cousin. Cousin Helen did not adjust to the long-term stay and returned home. Next, cousin Rita, a younger daughter, stayed on after the summer season. She would become a permanent member of the Sandlass family. Rita felt a kinship with Aunt Helen, Uncle Billo (Will) and cousin Henry that lasted a lifetime as a permanent member of their family often traveling in the fall and winter months to celebrate holidays at the hunting farm in Virginia. A trip home to the Bronx was just a train ride away from the resort's railroad station in front of the Sandlass house at the beach. This began many years of the Smiths and Grandma Lynch spending summer months at Highland Beach. Mae

1918 Spanish Flu Strikes the Shore

The 1918 Spanish Flu raged through the Jersey Shore causing a quarantine in nearby Asbury Park on Oct. 8 after 1,408 residents were diagnosed with the flu that year in a city population of 11,372. This particular strain of the virus was imported into the United States through military personnel returning home on packed troop ships from the European battlefields of World War I. Schools, churches, theaters, pool halls, bowling alleys and clubs were all off limits in Asbury Park, Highlands and other local towns. Public drinking fountains were ordered shut off. Restaurants remained open with kitchen staffs ordered to disinfect utensils and dishes in boiling water after each use. In Deal, the Coast Guard station was "practically put out of commission" when six of the eight men stationed there became bedridden, reported on Oct. 14, 1918. In Bradley Beach, 100 people were diagnosed. In Neptune, there were 310 cases in one week. The police chiefs of Asbury Park and Ocean Grove issued a joint appeal to parents to keep their children in on Halloween night. The pandemic continued into early 1920 when news articles reported that cases of the flu were dropping that winter.*

* Larsen, "Jersey Roots."

and the children preferred the ocean ride to the beach. They would leave the city in June and travel by steamer, which departed lower Manhattan, a one-hour trip to Highland Beach. Frank joined the family on weekends. As the children grew, they began to participate in the many jobs that were part of running the resort. Helen, the oldest, worked many summers in the ice cream/candy store. Rita worked in the luncheonette and helped her aunt Helen Sandlass assist with arriving guests. Doris worked at the snack bar for many years. Francis was taken under the wing of his older cousin Henry doing odd jobs and repair work that the resort required. He also handed out bathhouse keys in the key room at the Bathing Pavilion and bartended in the Bamboo Room. Francis eventually came to live at the beach year-round, graduating from Leonardo High School. World War I was nearing an end in 1918. Will's mother Annie passed away in her son's home at Highland Beach in the early spring in her eighty-seventh year. Twenty-seven years had passed since her beloved fruit stand opened on the first floor of the Sandlass Pavilion showcasing the "farm to table" varieties at the shore.

Soon after Will's mother passed away, a "dry zone" was designated within a half-mile radius of the Sandy Hook military reservation, where soldiers were in training. No alcohol sales were allowed in the bars or hotels surrounding Highlands and Highland Beach. Immediately, signs for the sale of "near beer" were posted. Will Sandlass realized that a major source of revenue at the resort was at risk because of the surge in opposition to the sale of alcohol in public places, affecting the nation beyond Sandy Hook.

20

PROHIBITION YEARS

The Roaring Twenties exemplified a period of significant changes worldwide in both social and cultural trends and innovations. It was a period of economic prosperity and growth for the middle class in North America, Europe and many other parts of the world. It was commonplace to find automobiles, electric lighting, appliances, radio broadcasts and more. The Jazz Age began, and fashions changed to shorter hemlines and hairstyles. Women's suffrage was enacted in the United States in 1920. Contributions by women to the war effort brought them into the public arena. A new freedom for women was seen in bathing attire at the beach. The Janzten swimsuit line was in vogue. Bathing suits were made with a jersey knit in vibrant colors and accessorized with swim caps and bathing shoes. Sandlass Pavilion responded to the new fashions. It operated a beach store with display windows showcasing the new styles. A fee of $1.50 allowed visitors to rent a bathhouse for the day. The Japanese parasols kept ladies' delicate skin from being scorched by the sun. A parade of bathing beauties in their new and daring styles was captured in the Highland Beach Photo Gallery and in family pictures on the beach.

The nation's hotly debated issue of alcohol prohibition grew into a grassroots movement. The Volstead Act set the starting date of nationwide prohibition for January 17, 1920. It set down the rules for the federal ban and the types of alcohol permitted for consumption. Highland Beach felt the weight of this new law enacted to control beer and liquor supplies in many cities, including New York. Alcohol could still be used in medicinal

Baby Marie with sister Doris Smith next to their Japanese parasol in the beach style of the day. *Courtesy of the Frank Smith collection.*

prescriptions, church services and personal use at home. Throughout the summer, excursion parties still flocked to Highland Beach, where the combined Bamboo Garden and Airdrome theater had live music and movies. Highly publicized cinema shows delighted guests, while the media focused on celebrities. A regular billing, the musical bands from Rector's Restaurant in New York City still attracted fans.

Summer eventually turned to winter, and a record-breaking storm with ice boulders on the road became a sensation in February 1920 at Highland Beach. The largest snow boulder ever recorded in the state had a foundation of ice cakes hurled by the sea onto the railroad tracks in front of the Sandlass Bathing Pavilion. Left high and "dry" during the storm, some of the ice cakes weighed tons. A particular drift stood twenty feet high, two hundred feet long and one hundred feet wide. The drift had to be cut through by railroad employees to open a route for the trains running from Fort Hancock to Long Branch. After the storm, seven-year-old Henry Sandlass headed out to sled on a favorite hill in town where the train tracks crossed Miller Street in Highlands. A young girl ventured out at the same time. She was injured in a sledding accident at the train tracks and taken to Long Branch Hospital. Helen Sandlass, hearing of the accident, no longer allowed her only son to take his sled and trek back to Miller Street on snowy winter days.

As the twenties roared into the new decade, Will had a chance to realize his dream when the Highland Beach Improvement Company offered to sell him the resort. Will had overextended his business transactions at a very inopportune time, creating a temporary cash flow crisis to complete the purchase. On March 18, 1920, his Irish immigrant mother-in-law, Bridget Lynch, famous for saving her pennies, filled the monetary gap. Will, an accomplished card player and horse-betting man who didn't mind taking a risk, gave a promissory note with interest to Bridget. It was a matter of pride that he returned the favor in quick order.

As the new owner of the resort, two months after Prohibition's Volstead Act went into effect, Will found himself in the center of rum-running activity, known as Rum Row, off the coast near Highlands at Sandy Hook. Allan Dean of the *Atlantic Highlands Herald* wrote an article on January 3, 2018, about the rum-running era. This excerpt notes the effect it had on the small town of Highlands:

> *While the Act, which banned intoxicating liquors to everyone in America, was later recognized as a 14-year social experiment it ended with the passage of the 21st amendment, which made it legal to drink again.*
>
> *But along the Shrewsbury River, the Bayshore waterway that opened out to the Atlantic Ocean, the seafaring men who made their daily living fishing, clamming, lobstering and boat building, became the bootleggers, rum runners and smugglers who catered to the needs of a thirsty nation by night. The age of the rum runner was a lively time for Highlands…all these folks were dealing outside the law, so in addition to keeping out of reach of law enforcement, they also faced dangers and death from others dealing in their same trade. These were the hijackers, those who made their living by stealing from the bootleggers.*[58]

An anonymous rumrunner shared his adventures, "Confessions of a Rumrunner," in the book *Stories from Highlands, New Jersey: A Sea of Memories* by John King. The rumrunner told the story of five or six boats that formed combinations and worked as an "outfit," landing loads of liquor right through the surf in rowboats at Sea Bright. When the returning boats rounded the Hook, other boats that had been hiding out in the darkness and without any liquor would speed out as decoys for the U.S. Coast Guard patrol boats and trick them to follow as far as Staten Island. Meanwhile, the boats with liquor headed to their landing places and unloaded their cases.[59] During the years when alcohol was not allowed, the Bamboo Bar sign at the resort came down and was replaced with "The Cafe" signage to signal a change. Located next to the seawall and boardwalk, this spot was frequented by thirsty beachgoers to refresh themselves with orangeade and lemonade. The lines were long when Will's brother Johnson held court at the new refreshment stand. He presented large "jugs" of lemonade on the countertop, where he created special recipes to flavor the drinks. In King's *Stories from Highlands, New Jersey*, Ann McNeil in 1989 recounted: "Prohibition made so many changes in our peaceful little town….Often I woke in the night to the sound of gunfire and wondered what neighbor's son would not be coming home next day. One such case was a young man….He left a wife and child."[60]

As the summer turned into the month of July, the thirteenth America's Cup Challenge held viewers enthralled. This contest was the last one in which the yachts competed in the New York Harbor and Sandy Hook Bay. The *Shamrock IV* of the Royal Ulster Yacht Club vied for the cup against *Resolute* of the New York Yacht Club in the best-of-five contest. It was reported that a huge throng of close to seventy-five thousand people on the beaches along the seacoast from Highlands to Asbury Park witnessed the event on July 26, 1920. Carrying American flags, the fans vigorously waved at the yachts. In the first hour, the contenders came so close to shore near Highland Beach that thousands of automobiles and visitors were attracted to the event along the coast. The winner was *Resolute*!

The evolution of Highland Beach went forward in spite of Prohibition and transportation challenges. Even though the highest rate of train passengers to the shore occurred in 1920, cars would be preferred over the next thirty years. The number of autos and poor road conditions were complicated by the lack of parking spaces. The ability to accommodate the cars that were increasing at an astounding rate for the small space available on the resort grounds compounded the situation. In his documentary, Chris Brenner recounts: "By the late 20's the transportation load had inverted, with more visitors arriving by car instead of train and boat. The traffic caused large backups in the area, and parking was a daily problem….The explosion of automobiles and roads forced some of the local trolley lines to shut down as more emphasis was put on roads and bridges to accommodate all the cars. Sandlass upped the level of decor and services, adding a spa and hairdresser, as well as other visual improvements."[61]

One of the local stars, Gertrude Ederle (Trudy), the "Queen of the Waves," spent summers in Highlands. Trudy made headlines when she

The Shrewsbury River, a training ground at Highlands and Highland Beach for Gertrude Ederle, the first woman to swim the English Channel, 1926. *Author's collection.*

became the first woman to swim across the English Channel in 1926. An American competitive swimmer and Olympic champion, she was taught to swim in Highlands by her father during the time their family spent visiting their family-owned summer cottage. There were countless hours spent in the water between Highlands and Highland Beach in the Shrewsbury River. It was recounted that the small girl's father tied a rope around her waist to set her off into the river. Soon, by all accounts, she was outdoing the boys in speed and distance. Trudy's sports legacy spread far and wide, with honors in the International Swimming Hall of Fame (1965) and the National Women's Hall of Fame (2003). Trudy would stay true to her roots in the Highlands over the years, often participating in civic events and presenting local swim team awards for youth at Sandlass Beach. A memorial park in Trudy's memory is located at the base of the bridge leading to Bay Avenue in Highlands. These words convey her spirit inspired by the sea: "To me, the sea is like a person…like a child that I've known a long time. It sounds crazy, I know, but when I swim in the sea I talk to it. I never feel alone when I'm out there."[62]

An object of curiosity appeared on the sands of Highland Beach in July 1926. An ornamental wooden Indian was taken early one morning from the front of Mr. Gold's store in Fair Haven. It was flung into the river and floated downstream until it reached the river in front of Highland Beach. A few men pulled it out of the water and set it up on the beach, where children were found playing with it as the owner arrived to retrieve it. The noble Native American had been seen floating down the river by a few people, who gave the news to the local paper. The train passengers and crew found it a curiosity as they approached the Highland Beach station. In spite of the damage from the rough trip downriver to the former Lenape camping grounds, Mr. Gold returned it to his store with a warning to those who had stolen it on a lark. The Cigar Store Indian, a Fair Haven landmark, was now tethered to a concrete base after it was returned to the happy residents in its village.

Each season, unexpected threats to the resort occurred as the months grew closer to the opening of the Bathing Pavilion on Decoration Day (Memorial Day). Fires and storms were still ever-present dangers at the shore, taking a toll on lives and finances. At the north end of the property, the summer bungalows had become more permanent. At its peak, there were twenty-five tenants' homes on "Dock Street," the main artery running down the center of the Bungalow Colony. Houseboats were often allowed to moor near the summer cottages. Preparations for the upcoming summer were underway when a fire from an unknown source erupted on May 25, 1927. One of the three bungalows owned by Will Sandlass in the Bungalow Colony on the resort property burst into flames. Each bungalow rented for $300 during the season to out-of-town guests. Three men occupied one of the cottages when the fire erupted. It spread to the two additional bungalows and threatened the carousel building. Flames jumped onto the roof of the Bathing Pavilion, where they were contained by the firemen called to the blaze. The man who ran the carousel was so grateful that he offered the firemen free rides. Many of them accepted, and they soon became sick from too many turns on the amusement ride. The $3,000 damage was fortunately covered by insurance. Once again, on warm summer days, carousel music infused energy into the crowds at Sandlass Pavilion. The business was humming along until the stock market crashed in 1929 and the Great Depression set in.

21

GREAT DEPRESSION YEARS

Undoubtedly, the Great Depression had a serious effect on Highland Beach, as it did on so many businesses at the time. Around 1930, the resort name was changed to "Sandlass Baths," and the amenities and amusements began a transition in response to the popular culture of the new generation. At the core of this new trend was the popularity of jazz music and movies from Hollywood. Even though the devastating effects of the Depression brought a new American experience, the sons of Will Sandlass were ready to respond. Will Sandlass's first son, Bill, had been operating the Sandlass Bros. Bathing Pavilion in Sea Bright from 1915 to 1923. He gave up his lease on the "Sandlass Bros." nestled between the Sea Bright Beach Club and the Peninsula House Hotel. The club, locally known as "SBBP," would later adjust its name to the Sea Bright Bathing Pavilion. (Today, it is known as the Chapel Beach Club.) In 1924, Bill was ready to own his own bathing pavilion business when he built the Sand Lass Beach Club on Ocean Avenue in Sea Bright between Sandy Hook and the Sea Bright town center.

Despite the Depression, new forms of cultural expression flourished and both commercial and New Deal programs were funded, affecting the shore. One of those programs funded by the state of New Jersey came to the Highland Beach area. In spite of scarce money, the state planned a new bridge between Highlands and Highland Beach. The low bridge caused a problem for boats passing underneath it, resulting in impossible traffic-delays. The nearby highway had been recently paved, resulting in an extraordinary increase in automobiles. This forced a decision:

> *By 1932, public works were underway in grand scale. The automobile traffic was intense, and so the State of New Jersey built a new "Million Dollar Bridge" across the Highlands narrows. The walking bridge was torn down, but the rail bridge remained in place. The new car bridge featured a split lift opening and a higher roadway to accommodate marine traffic.*
>
> *Construction of the new bridge caused dramatic changes to Highland Beach, however. The Surf House Hotel and Basket Pavilion had to be torn down to make room for the landing ramp of the bridge. The new bridge also pointed cars toward Sea Bright, adding a slight turning obstacle for visitors arriving from the West.*[63]

Another outcome of the Depression and the looming prospect of World War II put many beach development projects on hold and affected revenue up and down the shore. The result was a decrease in visitors and revenue. The idea of a national park at Sandy Hook had been discussed during this period. A reporter from the *Daily Record* in Long Branch interviewed Sandlass in the early 1930s and he gave his opinion of the plans for a national park:

> *I met William Sandlass, of Highland Beach, yesterday and he was bubbling over with smiles. "If you had asked me a month ago what kind of season was in sight," said he, "I would have replied: Things do not look so good." But now it's different. I have had the best bathing business for June in the past 15 years. Crowds were never so large and last Sunday broke all records. Mr. Sandlass is a unique character at Highland Beach. Not everybody knows the latter is a part of the borough of Sea Bright, the extreme northern end, but it is and William Sandlass monarch of all he surveys. If the residents there had the selection of a man for mayor, Sandlass would win in a walk. He has served in the Sea Bright Town Council and is well versed in municipal affairs. "Sandlass Beach" is a mighty interesting place, and no one would be happier than William Sandlass if Sandy Hook was chosen as a national park in 1932.*[64]

A petition was presented to the U.S. Congress to create a National Park at Highlands and the oceanfront. Following a review, the lands were considered too small. The plan was defeated and the idea abandoned.

Relief came to the operation of Highland Beach when Prohibition ended in 1933 and the Twenty-First Amendment to the Constitution was passed and ratified. Life continued at the beach, with family members building memories that would be told years later. As time passed and Will's second son, Henry Sandlass, and his cousin Fran Smith grew into adolescents, they both began participating in many of the tasks associated with operating the resort under the supervision of Will. During the off-hours, the Smith and Sandlass families relaxed with their children. A trapdoor in the Surf House hotel served as a diving hatch to drop into the river and swim off with the tide. In the mid-1930s, the Bowling Alley at Highland Beach had long been in disuse. The single-story Bowling Alley extension on the house along the tracks and the seawall was still there and was used mostly for storage. Teenage Henry and younger cousin Fran pretty much had the run of the place. After a long day of work, once all the patrons had left for the day, one of them came across the long-forgotten pins and bowling balls after the sport fell out of favor. They decided to bring them over to the row of bathhouses. The lockers were now empty for the day, with no one around. They set up the pins on the long central alley of the bathhouses. They proceeded to launch the bowling balls the full length of the bathhouses (probably two or three times the length of a normal bowling alley). They wanted to see how good they could get at their newfound "sport": bathhouse bowling!

There were days when the Smith cousins went into New York City. One summer evening at sundown, Fran and his younger brother Mickey were due to arrive on the train near the hotel. Sitting on the hotel porch, the family awaited their arrival. Being closer to home before the train arrived at the nearby station, the two travelers jumped off the train in the middle of the tracks, only to look up and see an oncoming train approaching. Fran pushed Mickey down the hill, and they arrived safely in front of their parents' eyes.

In the 1930s, Highlands had a population of encampments that housed Gypsy families. A well-known woman, Madame Stanley, and her Gypsy (Roma) family camped across from the Highlands train station near Portland Road. Her husband was a woodworker who made furniture for local residents. The Roma families camped in Highlands, Atlantic Highlands and Leonardo. They went to state fairs and gave demonstrations of wood carvings. One day at Highland Beach, a Gypsy man named Jim struck up a conversation with Henry's cousin Fran. It fascinated him when the Roma man took out a peach pit and carved a small monkey as a gift. Somewhere in time, the little monkey was lost in the sand.

Crowds came every summer when families spent time relaxing together. Once they arrived, there would be a crush of people paying admission and getting a key to a locker or a bathhouse. When the former glory of the

Bamboo Garden had faded, the four-towered original carousel building with the large dome was converted to the men's locker room annex. Will Sandlass purchased a truckload of wooden lockers from a New York City hotel that were slated for demolition. They were installed around the walls of the emptied-out Bamboo Garden/carousel building with one exception: still standing in the center, reaching up to the heights of the central dome, was the original preserved coconut palm tree that Will Sandlass purchased and had shipped from Cuba along with the trainload of bamboo in 1908.

All of these changes had taken its toll on the aging Will Sandlass. His health started to decline in 1935. His son Henry left Holy Cross college at the end of his sophomore year to take over operations at Sandlass Baths assisting his mother, Helen. By November, another storm had caused heavy damage to the Sandlass establishment and it was almost completely destroyed. Major renovations rather than improvements were on the way. The Bathing Pavilion took on a different architectural character when Helen and Will left on a winter cruise. Henry and cousin Fran were left in charge of business repairs. The beginning of a modernization in the new era had begun. The younger generation had plans for a much-needed renovation over the next few months. When Henry's mother and father returned from their winter cruise, Will was transfixed by the building's change. The second story of the Queen Anne building was removed and replaced with a one-story pavilion covered in tropical roof tiles. The veranda had been redesigned in a Spanish Colonial Revival style. Will's first concern was the fear that the clay roof tiles were so heavy they would crush the building. The new Sandlass Baths, Highland Beach Bathing Pavilion, had completed its first transformation, with more to come.

The buildup to World War II changed the priorities of the military at Fort Hancock regarding the road into the military reservation. Will's 1893 Bamboo Bar and family residence was encroaching thirty feet onto the roadway designated for the federal government's use. The government's original purchase of the land from the Highland Beach Association included this portion of the road, although it was never used. By 1936, the government notified Will Sandlass about the military's need to increase the width of the road. Even though Will's building had been on the roadway for forty-five years, it would have to be moved or require a court decision. The ensuing court action proceeded at a slow pace and would not be resolved in a timely manner. The Sandlass family faced the inevitability of a resort reincarnation that required the demolition of buildings to make space. Sadly, in November 1938, Will Sandlass passed away. His family had been on holiday at his

The SANDLASS BATHS Bathing Pavilion after conversion to Spanish Colonial Revival style. William Sandlass is on the veranda in front of the lobby entrance, circa 1935. *Author's collection.*

farm, the Shooting Box, near the Pamunkey River in Virginia. The *Atlantic Highlands Journal* on December 1, 1938, reported his loss: "Word has been received here of the death of William Sandlass, seventy-six years old, in Lester Manor, Va. Mr. Sandlass who was a pioneer hotel and bathing beach owner of Highland Beach, had been ill for some time."[65]

Will Sandlass created a trust as part of his will that allowed Helen and son Henry to run the business. A court decision to determine the fate of the Bamboo Bar and residence was further delayed. The family would wait two years for a resolution to the encroachment as the current business prospered. Another summer delivered excitement. News reports noted that fifty children had gathered along the road at the resort to welcome the King and Queen of Britain as they went by on their way to Fort Hancock. On June 10, 1939, King George VI and Queen Elizabeth motored from Red Bank station down Rumson Road to Sea Bright, past Highland Beach on its way into Fort Hancock to an awaiting destroyer, which took them to

New York. It was the beginning of a modern era on the southern end of the Sandy Hook peninsula when Highland Beach and Highland Beach rail station were renamed North Sea Bright in a resolution adopted by the Sea Bright Council in July 1939. The new address was Sandlass Baths, 5 Ocean Avenue, Sea Bright. The Sandlass Pavilion on Surf Avenue at Highland Beach had entered the modern era. The Depression was in decline, and America's neutrality in the face of World War II would vanish.

PART VI

Resort in a New Era

1940–1963

With over seven decades of providing summer fun for thousands of people, this place was nearly paradise for those who came here to rest and relax.

—Chris Brenner

The Sandlass Beach Club property, Sandy Hook, circa 1950s. *From left to right*: Smith summer cottage, Sandlass House, Bamboo Room, Bathing Pavilion and Bungalow Colony. *Author's collection.*

22
WORLD WAR II IMPACT

Still facing the uncertainty of a court decision on the Bamboo Bar's encroachment, life resumed at the shore and there was the prospect of new resort plans. In July 1939, the war was looming and the U.S. Army base at Fort Hancock started to surge. A widening of the road became evident as time passed and the military enlarged its capacity. Heavy guns and mortars were built to defend New York Harbor, while seven thousand to twelve thousand troops were housed at the fort, including members of the Women's Auxiliary Army Corps. There was an increasing problem when these men and materials had to pass through the military reservation gate on the narrow road that passed through the renamed Sandlass Baths resort. One building sat in its way and created a narrow width on both sides. It continued to impede the official traffic going into the fort. Even though Will Sandlass was gone, his spirit remained at the beginning of a new era. His wife and son were infused with the energy and determination to continue the evolution of the resort in a modern world. Henry and his mother, Helen, ran the business operations as the nation prepared for war. Lieutenant Colonel John Mulhern, a man who had recollections of Sandy Hook and the local Highlands area, reminisced during an interview with NPS historians. He spoke of Helen and his time as a young man working at the resort: "Helen, Sandlass' second wife…I think she knew everything that was going on in that place. She could walk like she was jet propelled. She was a terrific person, Helen Sandlass.…And as I said before she had her fingers on everything that was going on in that place."[66]

Henry had taken his father's place as operations manager when he became Helen's partner in the business. His leadership forged a new path to meet the needs of the public. Will's foresight in changing trends was reflected in his son's decisions to modernize the resort as an answer to the transitions occurring in transportation and the road expansion. Automobiles meant an increasing need for space on summer days at the shore. They discussed whether to keep the blueprint of the present buildings or seek additional space for parking by choosing an innovative plan. He drew on all the experience he had learned from his father and mother during the years he watched the resort grow. Plans moved forward in a new direction to completely transform the business model for the next generation of beachgoers at Sandlass Baths. The government lawsuit prevailed. The army won its case, and plans moved forward. A new identity was forged after this court decision was finalized to resolve the right-of-way dispute. Rather than demolish the 1893 storefront and residence, it would be the centerpiece of the modernization. Helen and Henry cleared the land on the river side where the Surf House and Basket Pavilion stood in preparation for the anticipated court decision. The Candy Store and Bamboo Garden also came down.

Since the 1920 purchase of the resort property was done without knowledge of the encroachment, the U.S. Congress approved a resolution to cover the cost of the relocation. Henry and Helen moved the structure to the river side of the property in 1940. Instead of moving the Bamboo Bar structure in one unit, the Bowling Alley was detached from the back of the Bamboo Bar/Sandlass residence and placed across the street in the location of the former Bamboo Garden and Candy Store. The bamboo wood in the Bowling Alley's new design was repurposed from the original Bamboo Garden. The South Seas style represented a revival of the famous Bamboo Garden conducted on the same spot. As Will had done with the timbers of the roller coaster, Henry conserved the bamboo to build his new attraction. At the time, a local news article reported that the new interior of the tropical cocktail lounge was fashioned after the Titchfield Hotel in Jamaica, West Indies, where the Sandlass family had visited. A local artist, James Allerdice, painted murals depicting the South Seas surrounding the walls of the dance floor. Palm trees adorned the room filled with bamboo tables and chairs. Stories from Chris Brenner's parents, Ted and Jill Brenner, revealed it became a favorite spot for tourists and locals alike. Music and dancing could be heard on summer nights. Thousands made memories there on warm summer nights.[67]

Mr. and Mrs. Schneider at the Bamboo Room cocktail lounge, anticipating an evening with friends, circa 1940s. *Courtesy of the John Schneider collection.*

After the Bowling Alley extension was removed, the front of the building that housed the original Bamboo Bar and second-floor residence was placed on greased logs. The house-moving crew rolled the structure from its original location along the seawall to its present site on the river side. Cousin Fran assisted Henry at the house to convert the 1893 building into a full-time Sandlass residence. It took some time to hook up all the necessary conveniences while the renovations were taking place. As a temporary substitute for plumbing in the house, a garden hose was sent through a second-floor bathroom window. Eventually, all the modern improvements were completed and the family had a finished two-story home. It is the only remaining building today. During the reconfiguration of the resort in 1940, the house was moved to the former Surf House grounds and the garden remained next to it at the former Basket Pavilion location. The garden, once started by Johnson Sandlass, who thought the location had potential when he found a tomato seed growing in an ash pile in the early days of the resort, remained in the same place. The garden had provided meals for all the excursion parties coming to the resort. Will Sandlass's granddaughter Irene (Duffy) drew a rendering of the 1950s garden surrounding the Sandlass house on the river side. Often the house was filled with the fragrance of red

THE NEW BAMBOO ROOM

Typical of the new and streamlined night spots is the new Bamboo Room located a stone's throw from Fort Hancock's gates. This completely "different" room is a carbon-copy of the room that has made the Hotel Titchfield in Jamaica, West Indies, the travelers' favorite stop. The south-sea atmosphere gives you that vacation feeling. Makes you think you're really in the south seas. Mr. Sandlass, father of the present owner, brought back the idea on a West Indies trip. The bamboo used in the decorations including the outdoor sign, is authentic West Indies stock.

—*Daily Standard*, Red Bank, New Jersey, June 20, 1941

and pink climbing roses, hydrangeas, marigolds, gladiolas and sweet peas. The fresh vegetables were still producing a hearty bounty that fed the family in the summers. The garden provided carrots, onions, radishes, lettuce and tomatoes, which added to the summer meals. A playhouse was built for the children to match the colors of the Sandlass home. It was a daily meeting place for cousins and friends throughout the summer. The family often encountered Mr. Lusson, the German gardener who lived in the Bungalow Colony. He ensured that the vegetable garden and flowers thrived in the enriched beds of sand and salty air.

Dramatic changes surrounding the resort boosted the nature of this favored destination, continuing the success enabled by the foresight of its founder. Challenges were met as shifts in American culture affected the future of this beach community and the nation. The popularity of the automobile had caused a complete collapse of the New Jersey rail system in 1940. The Central Railroad of New Jersey eventually shut down the coastline service. The rail bridge over the river was dismantled, leaving the Highlands Bridge as the main thoroughfare to the resort. Travel by car was easier with the emergence of Route 35 and Route 36 along with gas stations and rest areas built to accommodate crowds on the highways. Sites farther south, like Point Pleasant and Seaside Heights, drew the attention of New York tourists who had other options when the new highways were put in place. Finally, the steamship lines ceased service to New Jersey, further cutting off access to the resort. At the same time, highways diverted many other tourists to southern locations in the state. All this led to further changes at the Sandlass Beach resort. Attractions like the second Merry-Go-Round faded. The building

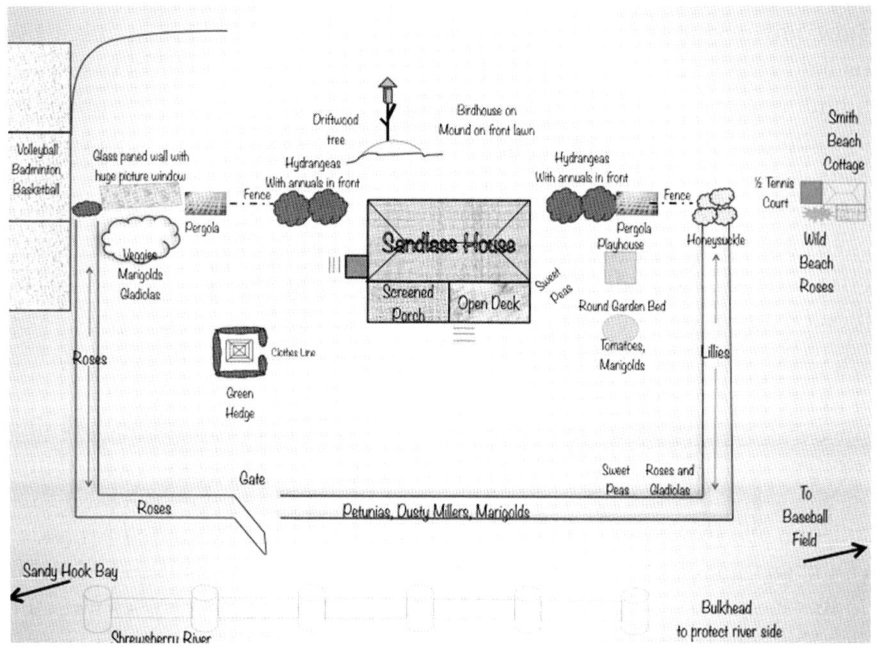

Artistic rendering of the Sandlass gardens in the 1950s as a re-creation of Uncle Johnson Sandlass's original Basket Pavilion, "Garden By the Sea," circa 1911. *Courtesy of Duffy Sandlass Cleary and Frank Smith.*

that housed the carousel by the bridge was turned into a summer home for the Smith family.

Excursion parties and day trips fell out of style, as basket parties and day visits by fraternal organizations were no longer in fashion. Even though the trains and steamboats stopped providing service to Highland Beach at Sandy Hook, the resort continued to thrive throughout the war years. Additional parking spaces were added on the land that was cleared when the larger resort buildings were taken down. Autos were the only direct transport to the resort at Sandlass Beach, except for occasional bus service in Highlands. The number of tourists being served on the premises shifted; instead, crowds were served in the expanding local communities with a more current view of a "day at the beach."

The secret of the resort's success was its ability to keep pace with the times. A family history of seeking new attractions and amusements enthralled visitors in this seaside location as a diversion from the demands of daily life. Events beyond their control had changed the future. Social changes again demanded a decision in the postwar period. Helen and

Henry responded as Will had in the earlier decades. His legacy of seeking new entertainments would be put to the test in times of increased austerity following the war. Helen and Henry faced a dilemma that required a bold decision. Remembering their travels with Will during the winters to seek new ideas, a previous trip to the Titchfield Hotel (Jamaica's first hotel built in 1905) sparked their imagination. Helen and Henry had redeveloped the resort around contemporary leisure concepts and family-oriented activities onsite. They aimed at a broad cross section of locals and, only secondarily, to tourists.

A reimagined resort arose on the landscape in 1941. The Surf House and Basket Pavilion, Bamboo Garden, Merry-Go-Round and Candy Store had disappeared. The latest diversions and recreational activities were centered around family themes popular in the 1940s. By shifting the resort's vision at the beginning of the wartime era, Henry Sandlass recognized the importance of a social transition appealing to a new generation and the emerging pop culture of jazz and swing music. Henry's tropical Bamboo Room and music venue provided a new entertainment option. It became a social epicenter of musical entertainment at Sandlass Beach.

Helen and Henry converted the Bathing Pavilion Reception Room, utilizing a bamboo theme similar to that of the former Bamboo Garden.

An evening of dancing in the tropical Bamboo Room bar at Sandlass Baths, Highland Beach, circa 1940s. *Author's collection.*

The Luncheonette was added with a Jamaican-themed screen porch facing the river and a tin roof that produced a waterfall on command, akin to a rainy day in the tropics. This transformation drew in the crowds. Autos were increasing on the property, straining the business to find enough space for visitors after a population surge in suburbia. Land was cleared to park up to six hundred cars packed with families on a summer day, allowing thousands of visitors to stream into the resort. The "Dock Street" bungalow colony at the far end of the bathhouses thrived. Hundreds of family members in the summer colony carved out their own identity throughout the summer. Dominick Mazzagetti's book on the Jersey Shore expresses many beachgoers' feelings: "Much of what we do and see at the shore today relates back to the pleasures originally enjoyed by beachgoers in the late 1800's and early 1900's—the sights, the sounds, the aromas, the food, and the games. We are linked to hundreds of past summers at the shore."[68]

The imprint of war on this peaceful strip of sandy beach took hold. One morning in December 1941, there was a knock on the door at the Sandlass home. Fran Smith was twenty years old at the time. He had spent another year working at Highland Beach, and when the summer season was over, his

World War II maneuvers by soldiers from Fort Hancock on the property adjacent to the Sandlass Baths, Highland Beach, circa 1941. *Author's collection.*

Above: Lieutenant Commander Henry Sandlass on a U.S. Coast Guard supply freighter in the South Pacific just before crossing the Equator on the way to Equatorial New Guinea. *Author's collection*.

Right: Boatswain Francis Smith in a Coast Guard promotional photograph during World War II. *Courtesy of the Frank Smith collection*.

aunt Helen Sandlass, her son Henry and Fran's sister Rita left the beach to go on a cruise, leaving Fran in charge. During a party on a Saturday night in early December, a number of the partygoers stayed at the house, where they slept until the next morning. It was midday when Fran awoke and looked out the front window to see to his amazement a large number of military personnel on the front lawn and throughout the resort. The Fort Hancock gate was only two hundred to three hundred yards away. As Fran recalls it, seeing this scene on the front lawn of the house, his first thought was, "Oh, no, what have I done now?" When he stepped outside to face his doom, he was told of the attack on Pearl Harbor that morning in Hawaii. His innocent youth and that of his whole generation had abruptly come to an end.

When World War II was declared, it also affected the remaining members of the Sandlass family. Highland Beach was a strategic location for military maneuvers. U.S. Army soldiers were bivouacked near the property adjacent to Highlands Bridge. In 1941, with the nation entering the war, travel and recreation took a back seat. Soon after, Henry Sandlass enlisted in the Coast Guard Officers Candidate School, leaving a leadership gap at the property. During the war years, Helen managed the business with the help of other Smith family members, who sustained the resort. Before deploying to the South Pacific in 1942, Henry Sandlass married Midge Sheehan. A year spent in St. Augustine, Florida, at a training school completed his preparation. Henry was sent to Papua New Guinea in the Pacific theater as a lieutenant commander in charge of a supply freighter. Fran Smith served as an enlisted man in the U.S. Coast Guard during World War II.

During the war years, the setting at this serene resort again belied the potential threat waiting in the ocean waters off the New Jersey coastline. The Sandy Hook coastal location suffered offshore attacks by German

SMITH FAMILY IMPACT ON HIGHLAND BEACH

The Smith family was integral to the growth of Highland Beach in the twentieth century. In addition, Mae and Frank Smith, the Sandlass' brother-in-law and sister-in-law, were a cornerstone for Helen and Will at the resort from 1913 to 1959. The six Smith children worked full-time summer jobs alongside their parents at the resort. During the World War II years, Mae and Frank assisted Helen while Henry was away over a four-year period. Their presence and work each summer laid a foundation for Helen and Henry to sustain the resort long-term both leading up to Will's passing and the following years.

submarines during World War II. These torpedoes in the waters off the Jersey Shore caused casualties that reached serious levels in 1942. Oil from sunken tankers left thick black deposits on beaches. State and federal help was necessary to remove the oil scum left behind. The deposits were shoveled up and the remainder buried in the sand or burned away. The U.S. submarine losses increased as it became evident the lights on shore were attracting the U-boats at sea. A coastal "dim-out" was ordered by the army. Beach towns sold special blackout curtains, and automobiles were not allowed to use full lights. By November 1942, the submarine threat was under control and the army ended the dim-out. Gasoline, sugar, meat, butter, cheese and canned goods were a few of the items limited by the government. Ration stamps had to be redeemed with each purchase. In spite of the struggling economy due to wartime shortages and rationing, families continued to spend time together in a seaside setting.

Numerous storms arrived in the Atlantic during 1944. The "Great Atlantic Hurricane" ripped into the Jersey Shore on September 14, 1944. The seventh storm of the year brought ferocious waves that washed away fishing piers and boardwalks. This treacherous storm raged across the beach towns leaving devastation in its wake. Severe flooding and waves reaching 40 feet threatened the coastline. The Sandy Hook peninsula suffered through

A swing band entertains the crowd at the new Bamboo Room nightclub during the opening year in 1941 at Sandlass Baths, Highland Beach. *Author's collection.*

this two-day deluge, bracing itself in 125 mile per hour winds. An *Asbury Park Press* article in 2017 by Erik Larsen recounted the horrific storm's impact: "During the storm's peak, the entire Highlands' downtown was swamped under five feet of water in the dark. At nearby Fort Hancock on Sandy Hook, the Army loaded up 15 trucks, including amphibious vehicles, and moved into the borough to offer whatever support it could as the town's bungalows literally began to float away."[69]

The North Sea Bright (Highland Beach) railroad depot, crushed by the storm, was later replaced by a passenger shelter. All the family members and the business survived the war. The future looked more peaceful as the war ended. Henry returned after four years of service to rejoin the resort business following September 1945. The changes to the property in the early 1940s ushered in a different feel. Even though the transportation infrastructure had changed, local crowds regularly filled the beaches.

23

MODERNIZATION

New developments affected life at Sandy Hook in the 1950s. The military installations at the Jersey Shore were expanded when the Korean crisis reached international proportions. By 1952, air-raid drills were implemented in Highlands following the fear of Russia's nuclear testing capabilities. The Cold War between the United States and Russia was escalating. In 1954, Nike missiles were positioned at Fort Hancock as a ground-to-air defense system against the possibility of high-altitude bombers. Beach erosion, another major concern for seaside towns, affected the most important asset at the shore. State aid provided for protective measures such as sand jetties to deter beach erosion.

Until this time, the Sandlass Baths, Highland Beach served day trippers and locals who filled the river and ocean beaches at the summer resort. The late 1940s middle class grew larger when the baby boomer population was born after World War II. This population explosion placed a new emphasis on the family. The difference was evident at the beach resort in this new era; the focus changed from adult excursion parties to family and child-friendly activities. As a new decade began in the 1950s, the resort's identity as a bathing destination was transformed. The business operation evolved into a private beach club for the ever-increasing local families. The conversion from a public bathing establishment to a private beach club opened the five hundred bathhouses to memberships during the summer months. The third name change, to Sandlass Beach Club, reflected the club's new identity, and it was quickly filled to capacity. Often, the members affectionately shortened the club's name to Sandlass Beach. The Bamboo Room cocktail lounge

Jerry O'Reilly and Norton Smith leased the Bamboo Room at Sandlass Baths, Highland Beach, circa 1950. *Courtesy of the Chris Brenner collection.*

remained open to the public as the "popular" night spot. As his father had done in the past, Henry leased the Bamboo Room to well-liked local men, including Norton Smith and Jerry O'Reilly and, later, William Hoag (a singer) in partnership with Dr. Louis Mellaci. Beginning on Decoration Day and throughout the summer months, Louis Michaelson's orchestra played nightly in the 1950s.

Generations of families returned on a yearly basis with children and grandchildren in tow seeking the enjoyment of a shared summer experience. Faces became familiar year after year as the children grew and families expanded, all wanting the same magic of a summer vacation in a favorite spot. Even though trains and steamboats had disappeared, the experience remained. Similar to his father, Henry Sandlass added activities by introducing some new sports attractions to the property, including side-street volleyball games (after hours), a tennis practice board, a softball field (evening games) and a croquet court (side lawn).

Families found pleasure in a multigenerational setting at Sandlass Beach Club. Sue Brenner Caffrey shared memories of summers in the 1950s (see sidebar "Three Generations).

Three Generations

Their story at Highland Beach began in 1904 when Alfred Kierschner rented, then quickly purchased, a summer home at 33 East Highland Avenue, Atlantic Highlands. Residing in the Bronx, Alfred was a successful executive in the leather-importing business, and the ferry service to Atlantic Highlands allowed him to have the family summer in New Jersey while he semi-commuted part of the week to the summer home. Until the 1940s, the family would often visit Highland Beach, as it was the premier beach resort in the area. They could either take the train from Atlantic Highlands to Highland Beach, or the family car, which had a driver who also stayed in Atlantic Highlands during the summer living in an apartment off First Avenue!

After the death of the Kierschners in the '40s, middle child Julie (Brenner) inherited the home, and during World War II, her young family, consisting of her husband, Bert Brenner, son Ted and, later, daughter Sue, moved to Atlantic Highlands permanently. In the years that followed, the family frequented Highland Beach, and by the late '40s, young Ted started working at the club as a beach boy for Henry Sandlass. He worked there through the early 1950s while attending both Red Bank Catholic High School and Manhattan College.

Another family, John and Mary Finn of Manhattan, had six children all being born in the late 1920s through the 1940s. During summers in the '40s and '50s, they rented a summer home in Leonardo and their children, mainly close in age, frequented Sandlass Baths during their teen years. The oldest Finn, Jack, dated and later married Mary Phair. The pack of friends they traveled with included Ted Brenner and Mary Phair's brother Art. Jack Finn's younger sister, Jill, was also included along with the other older Finns, Paul and Donald. Through these friendships spawned at Sandlass Baths and especially the Bamboo Room, Ted Brenner and Jill Finn became a couple and married in 1953.

The new family lived abroad and around the country while Ted was in the air force but returned to the area in 1959 rejoining Sandlass Beach Club (formerly Sandlass Baths) until the 1962 closing of the club. They then moved the membership to the "Sand Lass" at the Sea Bright location and remained members until the Sandlass family sold the property in the 1970s.

—Chris Brenner

Top: The Brenner family at Sandlass Beach Club, Sea Bright, New Jersey, circa 1950s. From left to right: Bert, Julie, Sue and Ted Brenner. *Courtesy of the Chris Brenner collection.*

Bottom: Alfred Kierschner and family at Highland Beach during the time they lived in Atlantic Highlands, New Jersey, circa early 1900s. *Courtesy of the Chris Brenner collection.*

Summer house rentals in the Bungalow Colony filled the cottages on Dock Street behind the bathhouses, including three cottages originally owned by William and Helen Sandlass. The icehouse had been converted into a cottage for a summer tenant in the early years. These families were also part of life at Sandlass Beach Club. The families who lived in the

A Fleischmann family picnic in the late 1940s near the bungalow owned by Lori's grandparents Bill and Sybilla Fleischmann. *Courtesy of the Lori Fleischmann collection.*

twenty-five beach cottages at the end of the property adjacent to the military entrance were an integral part of the resort teeming with community life. Edna Robinson Black was one of the Dock Street cottagers who grew up in a summer bungalow at Highland Beach. Her German grandfather, Louis Lusson, and her mother, Wilma Robinson, leased the renovated icehouse from the Sandlass family. Edna tells about the unusual cottage that once existed at the Highland Beach resort.

> *We took the train down and walked to the cottage. It was lined with burlap similar to a Merry-Go-Round with pictures painted on it and canvas on the floor and a round ring at the top. When there was a hurricane, sawdust came down. One day, Henry Sandlass, got a call to go pick up my grandfather. The military guard had arrested him. You know, he liked to walk down the beach. Without realizing it, he passed onto the military property. He told us he didn't know why they did that because he was a member of Coxey's Army* [a group of unemployed men who marched to Washington, D.C, during the depression year of 1894]. *The Sandlass family* [also] *owned the cottage next to us.*[70]

SANDLASS BEACH CLUB

My memories of Sandlass Beach Club begin at the age of four or five years old. I remember that my parents decided to accept Henry Sandlass's offer to take one of the new cabanas in the 1950s. We got the green one.

The adults had great parties on the cabana porch, lots of food and drink, and visiting. Us kids got to play on the beach and enjoy the goodies, and of course, we'd stay well into the evening! The Brenner family were members until the beach closed in 1962. My brother, Ted, worked at the club, along with his friend, Art Phair. Some of the other guys on the crew were Dick Nelson, John Kouwn, Neil Kouwn, the Peer brothers and in later years the Cullens, Billy Mulligan and many more. The first lifeguards I remember were Bucky Mass and Johnny Bell. Being an almost teen and then a teen at Sandlass was a wonderful experience. We had both the ocean and river beaches at our disposal. I particularly enjoyed riding the waves on the blue canvas and rubber mats the club had. You could only use them outside the ropes near Downsea. Even if the weather wasn't so great, we'd still enjoy ourselves on the screened-in porch behind the snack bar and Bamboo Room. You couldn't be there unless you bought something at the snack bar, so we'd buy sodas and make them last! Having friends who had summer houses on Dock Street at the Bungalow Colony was special. That was an amazing place to play. We were friends with the Koepchen family, who had the cottage right on the river. It was neat to sit on the porch, hear the water underneath and just watch the boats go by. Each summer, I'd get to spend an overnight with them. The bed was just like a bunk on a boat, and I'd be lulled to sleep by the sounds of the water underneath.

—Sue Brenner Caffrey

Mary, Gip and Rick (baby) Geffken at Sandlass Beach, Bungalow Colony at the resort, summer 1946. *Courtesy of the Rick Geffken collection.*

The former Highland Beach Association cottage was another summer home in the Bungalow Colony rented out by the Sandlass family. Through the 1940s and '50s, Edna and her family spent their winters in the heated Smith family cottage on the other side of the property.

Children were a focal point of the long summer days at the beach. Summer activities for families at Sandlass Beach Club included multiple generations in the fun. In particular, the children's summer programs were organized by a camp director, Ed Carton, and were filled with

BUNGALOW COLONY

Mary and "Gip" Geffken were married in April 1944 while both were still in the U.S. Army, stationed at Fort Myer in Arlington, Virginia. After their first son, Rick, had been born in August 1945, Mary lived temporarily in Jersey City with her mother, waiting for Gip to muster out of the service, which he did the following October. When they were honorably discharged, and before they found a permanent residence, they spent the summer of 1946 in a bungalow at Sandlass Beach. Mary described it as "the very last one on the road before the entrance to Fort Hancock." Living for the summer in the Sandlass Beach bungalow gave them the opportunity to think about finding a home.

Mary remembered that her cousin Grace Ritzinger, just fourteen, spent the summer of '46 with the young couple. Grace enjoyed the beach and made friends with other bungalow folks and young people in Highlands. Grace, more like a sister to Mary than a cousin, was Rick's babysitter on most Saturday nights, when Mary and Gip enjoyed time at the Bamboo Room, the hot spot just down the road from the bungalow colony. Grace and Mary would put Rick in a stroller on their weekly jaunts across the bridge into Highlands for grocery shopping. They spent the days on the beach after the morning's "domestic chores" were done. It was a happy time for everyone.

The Geffkens knew Henry Sandlass and especially his mother Helen (nee Lynch), who ran Sandlass Beach. Mary recalled Mrs. Sandlass as "quite a presence on the property."

Mary told some tales about a southern family living in a neighboring bungalow. Thickly accented, the mother's voice calling her children amused Mary and Grace and, no doubt, the other women in the bungalow colony whose husbands worked elsewhere during this summer just after the end of World War II.

—Rick Geffken

Henry and Midge Sandlass and their five children (Susan, Duffy, Ann, Hank and Sheila) at the Sandlass home in Sea Bright, New Jersey, 1951. *Author's collection.*

swim lessons and games culminating in awards and prizes at the end-of-season celebration. Gertrude Ederle, the world-famous English Channel swimmer who had trained in the waters at Highlands, presented awards to swimmers during the 1958 celebration at the conclusion of the summer. The children always counted on winning prizes in the many water activities and swim competitions at this special event. Fishing competitions lasted through the summer with cumulative prizes for the most fish caught in the summer months. The Sandlass family freezer overflowed with porgy fish (called scups in the early Highland Beach days). Greased watermelon races in the river can be seen in old home movies, showing one hundred children diving for a prize under the watchful eyes of their parents and friends. Social dances at the Bamboo Room, cabana parties and staff softball games on Sunday evenings captivated the members and their guests.

In the 1950s, Henry and Midge Sandlass raised five children on the property, in the same house that once obstructed the roadway into the fort and still stands on the property today. The five children—Susan, Duffy, Ann,

The Sandlass House

I so remember The House. Five Ocean Avenue. The trip over the old Sea Bright drawbridge and up the strip always seemed so long and yet so exciting and filled with so much anticipated joy. There were few beach clubs along that strip, and some of the houses and small cottages from back then still stand today after all of the years, and through all of the storms. Truly remarkable.

But THE HOUSE. I can walk you through it right now. An entrance area, the square tiled floor and that magnificent grandfather clock to the left side of the door. The beautiful pine-paneled living room with the gorgeous girl-with-the-horse-apple painting. The little office off of the end of the living room on the left, with a door going outside, and where there was another telephone! The screened porch off the living room, overlooking the river. A lovely dining room, where kids never ate (at least when I was there—until perhaps high school), and a kitchen which had a kid's playroom off of it, with A REAL BLACKBOARD! Just like school. It was magical.

During many, many weekends through our grammar school years, I was blessed enough to spend much time there. Ah, life was going to be great already. Susie and her four siblings were so much fun during those weekends, as we made up and played so many silly games, running all over that magnificent house. And when it came time for bed, I can remember falling asleep to the sounds of that grandfather clock as it played its magnificent Westminster chimes every quarter hour, and as the ocean waves crashed outside across the road. Magical indeed. Roller skating in between the cars in the summer, and it being so much easier when the season closed down. The cats, which never came inside, but were there to "take care of things" outside The House. The Bamboo Room, where we were never EVER allowed to go into as kids. Which made it even all the more intriguing and exotic. The playhouse and the cottage, where some of the Smith cousins would come and spend part of the summer, making the gang bigger and even more lively. Swimming in the ocean, going across the street and then swimming in the river. That's where the swimming lessons were held. Back in the day, there were hardly any beach clubs that had their own pools, so the river was a perfect spot to learn. Didn't Gertrude Ederle get her start in those waters? The Sisters of Mercy, graciously being invited by the Sandlass family each year, being on the beach WITHOUT THEIR HABITS! Still covered up, pale as ghosts and oh so shy, they were able to find the courage to shed their robes and go running, squealing all the way down to the ocean. At the end of the day, they went home happy as clams and red as beets. God bless them. The hurricanes, with their roaring ocean, could thrill you when you were brave enough to climb the steps to confront them and not be blown away, until they were too powerful and forced the family off the hook to find shelter at the Molly Pitcher, at our home or at other good friends' places. Five Ocean Avenue. THE HOUSE. Oh, The House. What wonderful stories it could tell. Oh, what a very special place.

—Julie O'Connor Collart

Hank and Sheila—immersed themselves in life at Sandlass Beach. There were opportunities to learn the business from a young age. Ann was often found sitting next to her grandmother Helen checking in members at the front office throughout the summer months. The next generation of cousins grew into their own responsibilities when Henry assigned tasks to even the youngest wanting to be part of the operations. Blackie Smith, a great-nephew of William Sandlass and Fran Smith's son, remembers summers spent at the Sandlass family's seaside resort as a six-year-old in 1960:

> *Walking the beach with my dad when he could visit, south toward Sea Bright along the water. Sitting in the kitchen, at the table, having a sandwich and lemonade, and looking out at the Twin Lights or the bridge going up to allow a passing boat to pass under it. A dress party in the Bamboo Room for six-year-olds, wearing a madras jacket and bucks and dancing with little girls in their party dresses. Being taken out with the lifeguards on the river. Visiting the workers in the key room. Walking from the Sandlass house, through the sand and the prickly sand burrs in the sea grass, past the play house to my grandmother's cottage.*[71]

SANDLASS SUMMER MEMORIES

Growing up on the Jersey Shore in the '50s and '60s was like experiencing a glimpse of heaven. Think *Cheers* but move the scene to Sandlass Beach Club and exchange the cast of adults for teenagers. Sandlass Beach Club was a privately owned club located on the peninsula, between the Shrewsbury River and the Atlantic Ocean between the town of Sea Bright and the Sandy Hook Naval Station. Most beach clubs were, and still are, privately owned except for a few public access sites. Days at Sandlass Beach were spent spread out on beach towels on the sand working on our tans, listening to music with songs by Elvis, The Beatles, Chubby Checker and others on our portable radios, and checking out the cute lifeguards. Sandlass Beach Club was unique because it was the only club that had an ocean beach and a river beach. So, if the ocean was too rough or windy, over to the river we went. From there we could often watch the local Highlands kids jump into the river from the bridge that connected Sea Bright to the town of Highlands. We were forbidden by our parents to jump from the bridge because of the danger of hidden concrete boulders beneath the surface of the river from a previous bridge. This, of course, made watching the divers even more exciting! The day usually ended with a double-decker strawberry and vanilla ice cream cone from the Bamboo Room snack bar for the ride home; probably the only way my mother could entice me to leave the beach! Until intrusions like summer jobs interfered with going to the beach, summers at the Shore always meant living the dream at Sandlass Beach Club.

—Pat Montamat O'Shea

Each summer, the beach club members looked forward to the Bamboo Room dances for teens and adults. Many teens spent their late afternoons in the Bathing Pavilion lobby, in front of the television, practicing the dance trends on *American Bandstand*. The yearly fashion show featured the latest styles. In the spirit of the times, the staff had softball games on Sunday evenings that brought out the crowds in nearby Highlands

Summertime in front of the Sandlass House and the Bamboo Room saw lots filled with cars seven days a week, circa 1950s. *Author's collection.*

to Kavookjian Field. The Holy Cross College alumni team's standing date each summer provided a friendly competition on the diamond. Parties followed on the beach at the cabanas. All through the summer, the screened-in porch at the Sandlass house played host to the end-of-year staff parties and local community guests far into the morning hours. When the Luncheonette conversion originally took place, the Quebec family leased it for the tourist season. During the next decade, the 1950s, John and Bunny Bell's Luncheonette in the Bamboo Room building was a popular destination for kids and adults. The delicious cakes, pies, cookies and ice cream were a big draw on hot days. They were delivered fresh each day. The candy store in the Luncheonette had a steady stream of customers. Hot dogs, hamburgers and sodas were the most popular items on the menu. The aroma of the grilled hamburgers wafted out the door all the way to the beach, drawing in standing room–only crowds throughout the summer. Rene Day shares memories of Uncle Henry at the Sandlass Beach Club: "Just a hot dog with chocolate milk. All I need now is the wooden screen door to the snack bar. One of my most

Above: The Sandlass House at 5 Ocean Avenue, Sea Bright, New Jersey, circa 1950. Original Fruit & Cigar Store/Sandlass residence at Highland Beach excursion resort. *Author's collection.*

Right: A pyramid of teens on the beach at Sandlass Beach Club, 1950s. *Courtesy of the Carolyn Mcmillan collection.*

A Cousin's Bond

Knowing that all our cousins were coming to spend the summer with us in the cottage meant Marie Smith would take us all out for a ride in her beautiful convertible to get ice cream on Saturday nights! Just being able to walk over at night to the cottage and hang out with everyone. Also, on rainy days we would practice the "Stroll" in the lobby of Sandlass Beach Club. Priceless! Best of all putting on plays in the playhouse with all of our cousins while our aunts and uncles looked on from the Sandlass porch.

—Sheila Sandlass Robinson

A Sleeping Giant

My most vivid memories of Sandlass Beach Club were spending every day of the summer swimming in the ocean or river, regardless of the weather or bathing conditions. Actually, it was usually swimming in both. In between, we spent time seining and fishing or rowing our rowboat, playing in our makeshift clubhouse, exploring the property and generally just hanging out with cousins and "summer friends" whom we only saw during the season. The Club offered a lot of outdoor and social activities, including swimming lessons, softball, fishing contests, dances and clambakes. The unusual aspect of living on the Club property was the contrast between hundreds of people enjoying the facilities for three months and just family and a few friends around during the other nine months. A contrast of extremes.

—Hank Sandlass

Christmas celebration at the Sandlass House filled with cousins in Sea Bright, 1951. *Author's collection.*

treasured memories is the sound of that wooden screen door and Uncle Henry handing me a glass of chocolate milk and a hot dog."[72]

Bathers sipping on ice-cream sodas and milkshakes filled the club's barstools and riverside porch above the beach to enjoy the sea breezes. Popular music played on the sound system piped into the restaurant while the patrons enjoyed their refreshments. A jukebox in the Bamboo Room filled the air with music day and night. The Bells and their summer employees worked at a feverish pace to keep up with the demand. John Bell doubled as a head lifeguard for many years. Tom Weber reported his memories in the *Asbury Park Press* on January 8, 2000: "When we grew older Connors, Bahrs, Aherns and the Bamboo Room were the places to go on Saturday night to meet friends, drink a few beers and dance the night away."[73]

Summer turned into fall. In early September 1956, an unexpected windstorm ripped off a portion of the roof at the back of the Bamboo Room. Sailing on the wind, the roof knocked down two utility poles six feet from the ground on its way across the road. Another season at the beach finished with a twist delivered by Mother Nature.

Sandlass Beach Club (Highland Beach) was a five-acre playground that went to sleep nine months a year and woke up in the summer. Some members called it Shangri-La, a reference to the earthly paradise that's protected from the ills of the rest of the world.

The resort may have seemed enveloped in a protective cocoon and insulated from worldly cares during the 1950s. But the sleeping giant awoke with news of the impending park plans at Sandy Hook.

24

POLITICS, EMINENT DOMAIN AND NEW JERSEY STATE PARK

Helen and Henry met the challenge of keeping Sandlass Beach Club significant and prosperous in modern times between 1940 and 1961. Even so, they could not stop the politics of the day. When the revived park plans pushed forward toward completion, it would forever change the southern end of Sandy Hook, where cabanas, bathhouses and restaurant amenities were provided. In 1931, these plans were viewed by Will Sandlass as a boon to Sandlass Baths, because an expanded park area would once again bring more tourists to the peninsula. In the 1960s, the federal government had another plan for the five acres nestled between the bridge and the entrance to a new park at the military gates. Public transportation had almost disappeared, and automobiles again created a challenge to the future of the business operation. As a result of its success, the overflowing number of cars parked at Sandlass Beach would be an impediment for traffic flow into the park. During the summer season, automobiles were located in every available space on the Sandlass property. The Sandlass parking crew acted as valets, positioning the cars side by side in multiple rows along the seawall, beside the Bathing Pavilion and in front of the Sandlass house and Bamboo Room/ Luncheonette. Additionally, hundreds of cars were parked in an extra-wide lot next to the bridge. Crossing guards at the beach club provided safety for the pedestrians crossing over the road from the river to the ocean side. Traffic gridlock remained a point of contention, as it does today. The bridge ramps planned at the time to ease traffic into the park

A Landmark For 75 Years

The 1950s were steady times at Sandlass Beach Club, with a family friendly club atmosphere. Swimming lessons, family events, and big crowds ruled the day, and business was solid. They say it's calmest before the storm, however, and 1960 saw the start of construction on one of the defining features of New Jersey—the Garden State Parkway. This high speed, limited access roadway opened up southern shore beaches for easy driving access from the north. Places like Lavallette, Long Beach Island and Seaside became the prime destinations for summer fun, and northern Monmouth County quieted substantially. At the same time, the State was starting to take over the southern half of Fort Hancock from the federal government, and they had plans for a large State park and beach on Sandy Hook. The State knew there would be large crowds and lots of traffic to use these pristine beaches never before open to the public, and that meant the need for roads and parking. Sandlass Beach Club stood right in the way — Chris Brenner, documentarian

would do little to alleviate the congestion. The storm clouds gathered in 1960, when Hurricane Donna devastated the area.[74]

The summer season in 1961 closed when state plans to acquire the land between the Highlands Bridge and the entrance to the proposed state park at Sandy Hook were confirmed. Helen and Henry waited for a notice from the state to notify more than five hundred member families who filled the space in the club's five hundred bathhouses and riverside cabanas. Negotiations had started and an offer made to Sandlass the previous April, ending in a difference of opinion over the value of the land. The state needed the land by 1962 for access roads to the park. When no out-of-court settlement had been reached by October 1962, the state proceeded with condemnation hearings to add the 5-acre tract to the 460-acre state park. The sun-filled days in the *Good Old Summertime* ended at Sandlass Beach Club when another era arrived. The New Jersey State Park Service opened Sandy Hook to the public in 1962.

In April 1963, following the yearlong court case, Helen and Henry Sandlass received notice to vacate all the property extending from the Fort

Sandlass Beach Club on a summer day without an inch to spare. Colorful umbrellas shield bathers from the unrelenting sun, circa 1950s. *Author's collection.*

Bill Sandlass (first son of William) at the Sand Lass Beach Club, built in 1924 at 825 Ocean Avenue, Sea Bright, New Jersey. *Author's collection.*

BOW TO PROGRESS

The state sued under eminent domain laws and in 1962 won a court case despite a hardy fight from the Sandlass family and many supporters. June 1, 1962, was the club's last day of operation. By July of 1962, Sandy Hook State Park opened, as demolition of some of the buildings on the site was completed. Other structures survived and were repurposed for a time, some into the 1970s. Most of the five hundred member families transferred their memberships to "The Sand Lass" club in Sea Bright (recently acquired by Helen and Henry), and many of the traditions and even furniture moved there. For seventy-five years, this magical location was a summer paradise for hundreds of thousands of guests. In many ways, this place launched the Jersey Shore tourism business, and the Sandlass and Smith families provided generations of service and fun to all who set foot...on Highland Beach....

Today, the land is simply a maze of ramps and bridges, unremarkable to most who pass through it. If you should find yourself driving along Route 36, or passing over the new Highlands bridge, maybe our story will help you imagine the laughter, fun and enjoyment that happened at this destination past.

—Chris Brenner, documentarian.

View the Highland Beach documentary at www.destinationspast.com.

Hancock entrance gate to the Highlands Bridge. Eminent domain had taken effect, and the Sandlass Beach Club, a landmark for seventy-five years on Sandy Hook, bowed to progress. Sea Bright mayor Thomas Farrell lamented the loss of Sandlass Beach Club in terms of the revenue from taxes alone ($300,000 in ratables, equal to $2,479,273.03 in 2019).[75] In March 1963, the *Daily Register* in Red Bank reported that the mayor beseeched Governor Richard Hughes to pass legislation for state reimbursement in a subsidy following the tax loss to the small beach community due to the Sandlass acquisition through eminent domain.[76]

Trifold postcard of Sandlass's Highland Beach, 1930s. Ocean and still-water bathing with ample parking space for those arriving at bathing parties via automobile. *Author's collection.*

The Sand Lass Beach Club owned by Bill (Will's son from his first marriage) still operated nearby on Ocean Avenue. Bill's retirement from the business afforded an opening for Helen and Henry to purchase the club in Sea Bright in 1963. The club remained in the family's hands through the mid-1970s. The Sand Lass Beach Club changed ownership and is known today as the Sands Beach Club. (A new club replaced the bathing pavilion after Super Storm Sandy in 2012 demolished the original building.)

In 1974, the Sandy Hook State Park was transferred to the National Park Service as part of the Gateway National Recreation Area (GNRA). Created by an act of Congress in 1972, GNRA includes New York City and Monmouth County. The South Seas Bamboo Room cocktail lounge became a maintenance storage area. It was lost to arson in 1978. The 1893 wood-frame Sandlass Pavilion House, original Fruit & Cigar Store and family residence, still remains in place after 127 years. On this small strip of land, the original timbers from the Gravity Switchback roller coaster are part of the building's frame. Currently, it is a vacant building. The Sandlass house stands as a Jersey Shore historic symbol representing the "Golden Era of Leisure Time" at the southern end of the Sandy Hook peninsula. Even though its time has passed, Highland Beach, Sandlass Pavilion played an important role at the birth of tourism on the Jersey Shore and contributed to the history of American culture over the seventy-five years of its existence. At the end of his life, Will was recognized as a hotel and bathing beach pioneer. His wife, Helen, and son Henry sparked the transition of Highland Beach, Sandlass Baths in the modern era. This new identity on the peninsula transformed the resort to retain its prominence as a vital asset in the seaside town of Sea Bright, New Jersey.[77]

"Immigrants," Lin-Mañuel Miranda sings, "...get the job done"

Rick Geffken's words reverberate in the Monmouth Roots, January 2017 publication of the *Monmouth Connection*. "Genealogists know that the daughters and sons of immigrants get lots of jobs done, the Sandlass Family of Sea Bright more than most."

Highland Beach, Sandlass Pavilion Boardwalk, circa 1893. Sandlass House/ Fruit & Cigar Store, Billiards and Bowling was the center of activity at the resort. *Author's collection.*

AFTERWORD

Several decades ago, when I was in my early fifties, I used to get up very early on late spring or summer mornings to go surf fishing in the Atlantic. (It was a lot easier for me to get up early back then.) I'd arrive at the mostly empty Sandy Hook beaches before sunrise, 4:30 a.m. or so, hoping to catch our ubiquitous bluefish or wrestle with elusive and famous striped bass. Occasionally, I'd walk along the Shrewsbury River side of the peninsula, too, where flounder—what we Shore fishermen call fluke—like to congregate.

I remember one day's adventure starting out at Plum Island and walking south toward the Highlands Bridge; not the huge parabolic span of today, but the previous one known as the "Million Dollar Bridge." (Like hundreds, perhaps thousands, of boys, I had survived the rite of passage of jumping from it.)

While casting my line and lot in the lee of that bridge, I gave little thought that morning of the old dilapidated house behind me. Nor did I have any idea then of my own personal connection to it, or that this ancient house was the very last remnant of a place where I had once lived as a toddler.

The Sandlass house was, by the 1980s, long past its glory days and was known by that name mostly to the family members who were raised in the two-story building. It turned out that I knew some of them—guests at my wedding—but these revelations were still years in my future.

Almost thirty years later, I was immersed in an effort to preserve and restore the Sandlass house. Susie Sandlass Gardiner, author of this book and direct descendant of the man who built her former home, enlisted me and several other local history enthusiasts to form a nonprofit group to publicize her grandfather's Highland Beach Resort. We were trying to restore and repurpose this shell of a building, the house Susie grew up in, the skeleton of which had been the first roller coaster at the north Jersey Shore. But you already know all about this remarkable story if you're reading this now.

We incorporated as the Jersey Coast Heritage Museum at Sandlass House (JCHM) in 2017, determined that the old place was worth saving and recognized by everyone. For the next few years, we gave it a good try, but government bureaucracy, the perilous location of the house itself and the enormous amount of money we would have needed conspired to prevent our success.

Nonetheless, we eventually partnered with the Friends of Twin Lights and mounted an exhibit at the museum within its walls with artifacts, images and videos about Highland Beach. Thousands of visitors to the iconic beacons at Twin Lights that had once shone over the rise and fall of William Sandlass Jr.'s unique vision have since learned about what a grand destination resort existed on Sandy Hook for the better part of a century.

If you asked our group of preservationists and amateur historians if the two years of meetings with politicians and Park Service personnel were worth it, you'd get an enthusiastic "You betcha!" And we'd all probably do it again, despite long odds against success. Why? For one thing, we discovered a whole lot more about a seaside recreation area where hundreds of thousands of people had frolicked in the sand and surf, escaping the heat and humidity of city life long before air-conditioning became the norm.

We're proud that the JCHM, however short-lived, also brought a lot of attention to the grandeur of escapist day trips at the turn of the twentieth century. Those steamboat, train and car excursions to Highland Beach, which became Sandlass's when its founder passed away in 1938, gave more pleasure to more people than just about any other little five-acre plot of land in New Jersey you can recall. And, in doing so, the resort helped the growth of Monmouth County not just financially, but also literally.

It's impossible to know how many visiting families, like mine, enjoyed the cooling breezes and warm sand in and around Highlands enough to move to Monmouth County permanently. However large or small the number, I'm convinced that Highland Beach/Sandlass's had a lot to do with those relocations.

My particular family migration to Monmouth County had its beginnings when my mother, Mary Cowan, first visited Sandlass Beach in the late 1920s when she was just a girl. She loved telling me stories about riding on the swing bridge—used by trains and cars!—over the Shrewsbury River as it opened and closed for boat traffic. (Apparently, the kindly bridge tender didn't mind giving kids a thrill just before a day full of them thanks to William Sandlass.)

The little girl was accompanying my grandmother Helen from Bay Avenue in Highlands to the well-known Highland Beach Resort in Seabright. You can imagine how cool it was for me to hear about my mom's seventy-year-old recollections about her own thrills on the bridge that preceded the one I recklessly threw myself from all those years later (and lived to write about it).

I know now that what my family experienced at Sandlass's was not especially unique. Lots of post–World War II middle-class strivers and their kids did pretty much the same wonderful things because of a visionary entrepreneur. So, we owe a huge thanks to William Sandlass Jr., his wife, Helen, and his son Henry for what they gave us.

The physical Highland Beach/Sandlass's may be only a memory now, but its legacy is firmly assured and well documented by Susie's Sandlass family stories presented herein. Embrace them while you can, because the Sands of Time, my lads and lassies, keep slipping by us all.

—Rick Geffken
Farmingdale, NJ

Appendix 1

THE EVOLUTION OF HIGHLAND BEACH TIMELINE

1881 W. DeForest, George Baker and Albert Townsend are early members of the Highland Beach Association. The association purchases seventy-four building lots at Wardell's Beach on Sandy Hook, New Jersey, and names this barrier spit Highland Beach.

1887–1890

Highland Beach excursion resort is erected and opens for business. It is the first and only "Excursion Resort" to offer both ocean and river bathing.

1887 Highland Beach Association leases lots 23 through 33 to Ferdinand Fish, president of the Highland Beach Improvement Company, for ten years with plans to create an excursion resort. Fish subleases a portion of these lots to William Sandlass for five years to begin the building plan.

1888 Eleven buildings exist in the blueprint for Highland Beach. In 1888, William Sandlass and the Highland Beach Improvement Company build bathhouses, several cottages and a shed pavilion. Highland Beach opens for business, and William Sandlass is listed as the proprietor. A railroad station is built and renamed Highland Beach.

1889 "Highland Beach...The New Excursion Resort" advertises the opening season. William Sandlass's Great Switchback Rail Road roller coaster takes the public to new heights at Highland Beach.

The Horseshoe Cove landing on Sandy Hook is the first stop for travelers on the peninsula. This year, all six small steam launches operate; they bring as many as three thousand persons a day to the resort.

1890 The first grand "Gala Day" draws thousands of visitors. Trolleys bring visitors from Red Bank and Eatontown with routes along the way to Highland Beach.

1891 A Photographic Studio is available for memories of a "day" at Highland Beach.

1892–1920

Golden Years: Hollywood arrives; yachting brings crowds.

1892 The steamboat-rail connection shifts from Sandy Hook to Atlantic Highlands. The Horseshoe Cove dock closes and moves to Spermaceti Cove on Sandy Hook. A new short rail connection to Highlands is built to allow direct train access to Highland Beach station across the newly constructed "criss-cross bridge" on the Shrewsbury River. The largest numbers are recorded to date at the resort when 125,000 people come in one season.

1893 The Great Switchback Rail Road roller coaster comes down. As part of the new lease, William Sandlass agrees to build the Sandlass Pavilion House (Fruit & Cigar Store). The roller coaster timbers are used to construct the Fruit & Cigar Store, Billiards, Bowling Alley and upstairs Sandlass living quarters, a two-story building on the footprint of the gravity railroad. The first pier is built at Highland Beach to receive steamboats.

1896 The Mel-Rah social club opens at Highland Beach.

1899 The start of the America's Cup Yacht Race is held in front of Highland Beach on Sandy Hook. The route between Sandy Hook and Long Branch sees thousands of people line the local beaches to watch the race. Marconi's first transatlantic radio transmission broadcasts the races from Twin Lights.

1908 William Sandlass arranges for a railroad car filled with bamboo from Jamaica and Cuba to be delivered to New Jersey. He creates the Bamboo Garden (Dance Hall), Airdrome and Bamboo Bar with the bamboo. The Bamboo Garden at the Sandlass Pavilion, featuring a full-grown palm tree in the center of the gardens, has live music. William Sandlass opens two additional social clubs, the Dar-He and Surf Clubs, between the depot and Sandlass property.

1914–1918
World War I

1915 Automobiles begin to open up the Jersey Shore for travelers.

1920 William Sandlass receives title by deed to lots 23 through 29 at Highland Beach.

1923 Trolleys stop running to Highland Beach.

1925 Highland Beach resort faces changes during Prohibition (1920–33). The liquor license at Highland Beach requires a shift in operations. The Bamboo Bar converts to a café. William Sandlass adapts to changing times by offering increased amenities for the day tripper. From the beginning, a spa-like environment is designed to encourage comfort and glamour.

1929–1939
The Great Depression

1930 The name of the resort is changed to Sandlass Baths, Highland Beach. In the 1930s, Highland Beach begins its transition into the modern world. During the Roaring Twenties, beach clubs become popular, offering families who can afford it a more exclusive summer experience. As the Great Depression begins, the iconic Highland Beach rebrands itself as Sandlass Baths and joins the modern trend.

1935 The Bungalow Colony thrives at Highland Beach. A series of bungalows are constructed over the years at the far end of the bathhouses. William Sandlass leases the property to the homeowners. Eventually, there are twenty-five bungalows on Dock Street at Highland Beach, located where the steamers arrive at the resort.

1938 A right-of-way dispute begins because of location errors in placing the Sandlass Pavilion House on the main road into the fort. The house encroaches on government property leading into Fort Hancock during the buildup to World War II on the Sandy Hook peninsula. William Sandlass passes away before the dispute is settled.

1940 The Bowling Alley is converted to the new South Seas Bamboo Room nightclub and Luncheonette. The Sandlass Pavilion House (former Fruit & Cigar Store) is moved to the river side of the resort and becomes a full-time residence for the Sandlass family.

1941–1945
World War II

1945 Steamboats stop running on the Shrewsbury River. Highland Beach train station shuts down following diminished train service to the beach towns along the route.

1947 Sporting Day at Sandlass Beach. Sports take a modern turn in the 1940s and '50s at Sandlass Beach. Aside from swimming and fishing, Henry Sandlass adds volleyball, a tennis practice court, a softball field and a croquet lawn for extra amusements.

1950 The "Trade Winds" begins a new decade at the Bamboo Room. Henry Sandlass leases the Bamboo Room to Jerry O'Reilly and Norton Smith at Sandlass Beach Club.

1951 Sandlass Beach Club transitions into a members-only business operation. A children's day camp, teen and adult dances, swim lessons, swim meets, staff softball team and end-of-year celebrations are added to the experience.

1962 Sandlass Beach Club is seized through eminent domain by the state of New Jersey and has its last season in 1961. The following summer, in 1962, it becomes part of the New Jersey Sandy Hook State Park property. The Sandlass Pavilion House is allocated as a residence for the Park Service. The Bamboo Room and Luncheonette are used for maintenance storage. The Bathing Pavilion (five hundred bathhouses), Smith Summer Cottage and twenty-five bungalows are demolished by the State of New Jersey for highway ramps and traffic access into the new park area.

1963 The Sandlass family moves from Sandlass Beach Club property to operate the Sand Lass Beach Club at 825 Ocean Avenue, Sea Bright, formerly owned by Henry's half brother Bill Sandlass. The 1893 Sandlass Pavilion House is all that remains of the Highland Beach excursion resort on the southern end of the Sandy Hook peninsula.

1972–1974

An act of Congress creates the Gateway National Recreation Area in 1972 under the National Park Service in New York City and Monmouth County.

1974 The state of New Jersey transfers Sandy Hook to the National Park Service. The park becomes part of the Gateway National Recreation Area in Monmouth County.

1978 The Bamboo Room and Luncheonette, a maintenance storage area, is lost to arson.

2020 The Sandlass Pavilion wood-frame house still remains in place after 127 years. Currently, it is a vacant building on Sandy Hook.

Appendix 2

ANCESTRY CHARTS

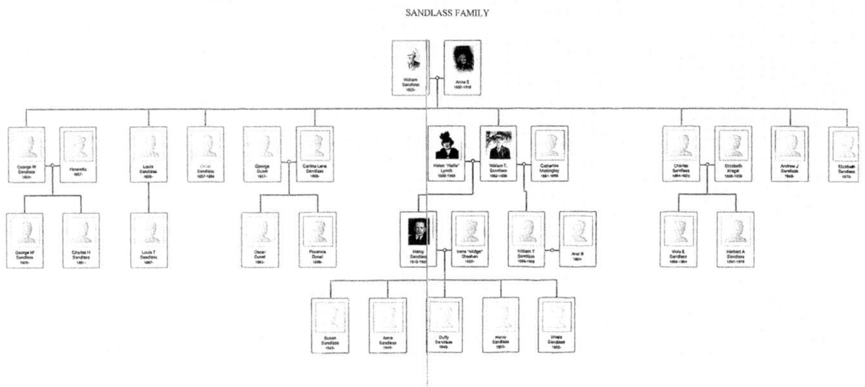

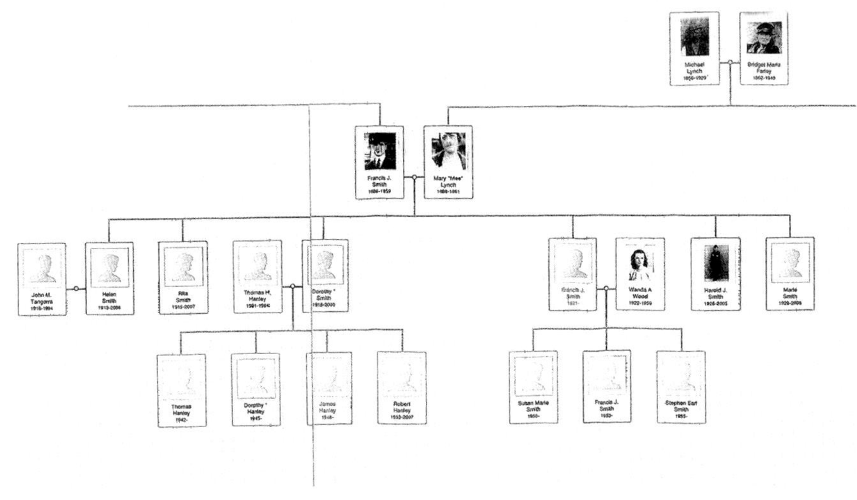

NOTES

Introduction

1. Houghton, *Sandy Hook in 1879*, 7.

Chapter 1

2. Brenner, *Destinations Past: Highland Beach*, documentary, 2017.
3. Howson, *Travel and Transportation*, 13.
4. "Big Improvements to Be Made at The Highlands," *Red Bank Register*, December 14, 1887.
5. Gabrielan, *Monmouth Beach and Sea Bright*, 7–8.
6. John Rogers Thomas, "Beautiful Highlands," M. Gray Plate No. 8101. New York Public Library, 1871.

Chapter 4

7. Rick Geffken, "The William Sandlass Family," *Monmouth Connection*, the official newsletter of the Monmouth County Genealogy Society (Monmouth Roots Genealogy Newsletter), January 2017, 28.

Chapter 5

8. Sheila Koehler and Margaret Westfield, "Architectural Styles at Highland Beach," email correspondence with Sheila Koehler, associate, Westfield Architects, August 20–23, 2019.

Chapter 6

9. King, "Notes on Highland Beach History," email correspondence with John King, historian/author, October 10, 2019.
10. King, *Highlands, New Jersey*, 80.
11. Kobbé, *Jersey Coast and Pine*, 9.

Chapter 7

12. "The Recent Terrible Storm on the Jersey Coast," *Frank Leslie's Illustrated Newspaper*, December 8, 1888.
13. "Highland Beach News," *Keyport Enterprise*, September 14, 1889.
14. "Storm Effects," *Passaic Daily News*, March 18, 1889.

Chapter 8

15. "Highland Beach," *Oracle*, August 1896.

Chapter 9

16. "Highland Beach," (advertisement), *New York Star*, August 1888.
17. Brenner, *Destinations Past.*
18. "Leading Event of the Season at Highland Beach," *Monmouth Press*, 1892.
19. "Camping about Highland Beach," *New York Times*, August 18, 1893.
20. "Gala Day at Highland Beach," *Monmouth Press*, August 1894.

Chapter 10

21. Thorstein Veblen, *The Theory of the Leisure Class* (London: George Allen and Unwin, 1899).

Chapter 11

22. "Camp Comfort," *Red Bank Register*, August 22, 1894.

23. "Highland Beach Flourishing Also," *Monmouth Press*, September 15, 1894.
24. Seebohm and Cook, *Cottages and Mansions of the Jersey Shore*, 14.
25. Mazzagetti, *Jersey Shore*, 94.

Chapter 12

26. "Gala Day at Highland Beach," *Monmouth Press*, August 18, 1894.
27. Brenner, *Destinations Past*.
28. "Sunday at Highland Beach: A Bigger Crowd Than at Other Time in Its History," *Monmouth Press*, July 25, 1895.
29. King, *Highlands, New Jersey*, 82.
30. "Summer Life in Sea Bright," *Standard Union*, 1895.

Chapter 13

31. Reussille, *Steam Vessels Built in Old Monmouth*, 152.
32. "Highland Beach," *Oracle*, August 1895.
33. "Highland Beach," *Monmouth Press*, June 6, 1896.
34. "Highland Beach," *Oracle*, 1896.
35. "Happenings at Highland Beach," *Monmouth Press*, 1897.
36. "Fishing at Highland Beach," *Red Bank Register*, May 19, 1897.
37. Ibid., "The American Biograph Company Consisting of 40 Persons Were at the Martin House Last Week," July 20, 1910.

Chapter 14

38. "Highland Beach," Monmouth County Historical Association Library and Archives, Freehold, New Jersey, 1899.
39. "Select Race Dates for America's Cup," *New York Times*, June 10, 1899.
40. Brenner, *Destinations Past*.
41. King, *Highlands, New Jersey*, 79.
42. Twin Lights Museum, "A Daughter's Memory," 2019.
43. "The Kaiser Cup Transatlantic Race," *New York Times*, May 16, 1905.

Chapter 15

44. *Red Bank Register*, "American Biograph Company," July 20, 1910.
45. Ibid.
46. Brenner, *Destinations Past.*

Chapter 16

47. King, *Highlands, New Jersey*, 83.
48. *Red Bank Register*, "Crowds at Highland Beach," July 7, 1909.
49. King, "Penny Postcards Preserve the Past," *Asbury Park Press*, February 2, 1997.

Chapter 17

50. Wilson, *Story of the Jersey Shore*, 83.

Chapter 18

51. "Aeroplane at Highland Beach," *Red Bank Register*, July 31, 1912.
52. "A Love Story in a Sweet Tale,"*Miami Herald*, September 29, 1912.
53. "Storm Damage at Highland Beach," *Long Branch Daily Record*, December 26, 1913.
54. Howson, *Travel and Transportation*, 57.
55. Brenner, *Destinations Past.*
56. *Red Bank Register*, "Shark Scare at Highland Beach," August 9, 1916.
57. John Mulhern, interview, National Park Service Interview, November 21, 1984.

Chapter 20

58. "Rum Runner Era," *Atlantic Highlands Herald*, January 3, 2018.
59. King, *Stories from Highlands, New Jersey*, 78.
60. Ibid., 79.
61. Brenner, *Destinations Past.*

62. Ederle quoted in Glenn Stout, *Young Women and the Sea: How Trudy Ederle Conquered the English Channel and Inspired the World* (New York: Houghton Mifflin Harcourt, 2009), 35.

Chapter 21

63. Brenner, *Destinations Past.*
64. "Sandy Hook State Park," *Daily Record*, 1932.
65. "William Sandlass Obituary," *Atlantic Highlands Journal*, December 1, 1938.

Chapter 22

66. Mulhern, interview, National Park Service, November 21, 1984.
67. "The New Bamboo Room," *Daily Standard*, June 20, 1941.
68. Mazzagetti, *Jersey Shore*, 230–31.
69. "Storm Damage at Highlands," *Asbury Park Press*, 2017.

Chapter 23

70. Gardiner, Edna Black Interview, June 2012.
71. Gardiner, Frank Smith Interview, July 2019.
72. Gardiner, Highland Beach Fan Page Comment by Renee Day, July 2019.
73. "Tom Weber's Memories," *Asbury Park Press*, January 8, 2000.

Chapter 24

74. Brenner, *Destinations Past.*
75. "Eminent Domain at Sandlass Beach Club," *Daily Register (Red Bank)*, March 1963.
76. Brenner, *Destinations Past.*
77. Geffken, "William Sandlass Family," *Monmouth Connection*, January 2017, 28.

BIBLIOGRAPHY

Books

Allaback, Sarah, ed. *Resorts and Recreation*. Mauricetown, NJ: Sandy Hook Foundation and National Park Service, 1995.

Boyd, Paul D. 2004. *Atlantic Highlands: From Lenape Camps to Bayside Town*. Charleston, SC: Arcadia Publishing, 2004.

Brown, Edward. *Just Around the Corner, In New Jersey.* Wilmington, DE: Middle Atlantic Press, 1984.

Buchholz, Margaret Thomas. *Shore Chronicles: Diaries and Travelers' Tales from the Jersey Shore, 1764–1955*. Harvey Cedars, NJ: Down the Shore Publishing, 1999.

Gabrielan, Randall. *Birth of the Jersey Shore: The Personalities and Politics That Built America's Resort*. Charleston, SC: The History Press, 2015.

———. *Images of America: Monmouth Beach and Sea Bright*. Charleston, SC: Arcadia Publishing, 1998.

———. *Images of America: Sandy Hook*. Charleston, SC: Arcadia Publishing, 1999.

Gallo, Tom. *Henry Hudson Trail: Central Railroad of New Jersey's Seashore Branch*. Charleston, SC: Arcadia Publishing, 1999.

Geffken, Rick, and George Severini. *Lost Amusement Parks of the North Jersey Shore*. Charleston, SC: Arcadia Publishing, 2017.

Hoffman, Thomas J. *Deeds of Sandy Hook: 1847–1972*. Fort Hancock, NJ: National Park Service, 2004.

———. *Fort Hancock*. Charleston, SC: Arcadia Publishing, 2007.

Houghton, George. *Sandy Hook in 1879.* Silverthorne, CO: Vista Books, 1998.

Howson, Jean. *Travel and Transportation at Highlands and Highland Beach, New Jersey.* Parsippiny, NJ: RBA Group, 2010.

King, John P. *The Highlands.* Dover, NH: Arcadia Publishing, 1995.

———. *Highlands, New Jersey.* Charleston, SC: Arcadia, 2001.

———, ed. *Stories from Highlands, New Jersey: A Sea of Memories.* Charleston, SC: History Press, 2012.

Kobbé, Gustav. *The Jersey Coast and Pine: An Illustrated Guide-book with Road Maps.* Baltimore, MD: Gateway Press, 1970.

Leonard, Thomas H. *From Indian Trail to Electric Rail.* Atlantic Highlands, NJ: Atlantic Highlands Journal, 1923.

Mazzagetti, Dominick A. *The Jersey Shore: The Past, Present and Future of a National Treasure.* New Brunswick, NJ: Rutgers University Press, 2018.

Methot, June. *Up & Down the Beach.* Navesink, NJ: Whip Publishers, 1988.

———. *Up & Down the River.* Navesink, NJ: Whip Publishers, 1980.

Moss, George H. *Another Look at Nauvoo to the Hook.* Sea Bright, NJ: Ploughshare Press, 1990.

———. *The Early History of Sea Bright.* Sea Bright, NJ: Ploughshare Press, 1972.

———. *Early Views of the Twin Lights and the Highlands of Navesink.* Sea Bright, NJ: Ploughshare Press, 1996.

———. *MONMOUTH Our Indian Heritage.* Town of Ocean, NJ: Roy Press Printers, 1974.

———. *Nauvoo to The Hook.* Locust, NJ: Jersey Close Press, 1964.

———. *Steamboat to the Shore.* Sea Bright, NJ: Ploughshare Press, 1972.

———. *Twice Told Tales.* Sea Bright, NJ: Ploughshare Press, 2002.

Reussille, Leon. *Steam Vessels Built in Old Monmouth: 1841–1894.* Red Bank, NJ: L. Reussille, 1975.

Roberts, Russell, and Richard Youmans. *Down the Jersey Shore.* New Brunswick, NJ: Rutgers University Press, 1994.

Savadove, Larry, Margaret Thomas Buchholz and Scott Mazzella. *Great Storms of the Jersey Shore.* West Creek, NJ: Down the Shore Publishing, 2019.

Seebohm, Caroline, and Peter C. Cook. *Cottages and Mansions of the Jersey Shore.* New Brunswick, NJ: Rivergate Books, 2007.

Wilson, Harold F. *The Story of the Jersey Shore.* Princeton, NJ: D. Van Nostrand Company, 1964.

Newspapers and Magazines

Atlantic Highlands Herald
Atlantic Highlands Journal
Asbury Park Press
Baltimore Sun
Courier-News (Bridgewater, NJ)
Daily Register (Red Bank, NJ)
Daily Standard (Red Bank, NJ)
Daily Times (New Brunswick, NJ)
Edge Magazine
Keyport Weekly
Long Branch Daily Record
Monmouth Democrat
Monmouth Health and Life
Monmouth Inquirer (Freehold, NJ)
Monmouth Journal
Monmouth Press
New York Evening World
New York Times
New York Tribune
Oracle: Highlands of Navesink
Passaic Daily News
Red Bank Register
Sandy Hook's Lifesavers
Standard Union (Brooklyn, NY)
Wolverton Atlas of Monmouth County, New Jersey

Online Resources

Ancestry.com. www.ancestry.com.

Architectural Styles of America and Europe. "Queen Anne." www.architecturestyles.org.

Art History Archive. "History of Postcards." www.arthistoryarchive.com.

Atlantic Highlands Historical Society. http://www.ahhistory.org.

Borough of Atlantic Highlands, New Jersey. "History of Atlantic Highlands." http://www.ahnj.com.

Borough of Monmouth Beach, New Jersey. Monmouth County Historical Association. https://www.monmouthhistory.org.

Borough of Rumson, New Jersey. "Historic Preservation Commission." www.rumsonnj.gov.

Change.org. "You Can Save the Last Historic Piece of the By-gone Era of the Jersey Shore!!!" www.change.org.

Coney Island Timeline. www.westland.net.

Duhart, Bill. "N.J. Beach Was the Only One That Allowed Black Tourists, but They Made It a Hip Place to Be." NJ.com. www.nj.com.

Edge 9, no. 1 (2017). www.edgemagonline.com.

Encyclopedia.com. "Urbanization of Leisure." www.encyclopedia.com.

Facebook. "Highlands, New Jersey." www.facebook.com.

———. "Twin Lights Historical Society." www.facebook.com.

Gandhi, Lakshmi. "The Extraordinary Story of Why a 'Cakewalk' Wasn't Always Easy." Code Switch. December 23, 2013.

Gateway National Recreation Area. "Fort Hancock and Sandy Hook Proving Ground National Historic Landmark." www.nps.gov.

Geffken, Rick. "Sea Bright's Seawall Saved More Than the Town." *Two River Times*, September 19, 2016.

Google Maps. "Jersey Shore." https://www.google.com/maps/d/u/0/viewer?msa=0&mid=1svKDzhtgTlYJaX5GDhWbeblgLS4&ll=39.98934210242604%2C-74.395144821141 57&z=10.

Highland Beach clippings. 1901. Dropbox folders. www.dropbox.com/sh/zr645vcw593vahl/AADHeqECRHLq5HljOdI-vZZ-a?dl=0.

———. 1942–1962. Dropbox folders. www.dropbox.com/sh/kxwva3umml7bblx/AAAIjUxBzSTF16EN0wrKAyd3a?dl=0.

Highland Beach Documentary by Chris Brenner. *Destinations Past: Highland Beach*. 2017. www.destinationspast.com

Highlands. "The Highlands, N.J. Timeline." www.highlandsnj.com.

———. "Postcard Archive." www.highlandsnj.com.

———. "The Story of Highlands." www.highlandsnj.com.

Historical Society of Highlands. www.highlandsborough.org.

Jersey Coast Heritage Museum. https://jchmorg.me.

Jersey Shore Scene. "Twin Lights Connection to Marconi." www.jerseyshorescene.com.

Kahn Academy. "Development of the Middle Class." www.khanacademy.org.

Keenbug: An Unencyclopedic History. "Keansburg Steamship Company." http://keenbug.blogspot.com.

Kelly, Greg. "'Wooden Palaces' of Monmouth Beach." Monmouth Beach Life. www.monmouthbeachlife.com.

Kensett, John Frederick. *Shrewsbury River—New Jersey*. Painting. Fine Art America. www.fineartamerica.com.

Larsen, Erik. "Jersey Roots: How the Spanish Flu Led to a Quarantine of Asbury Park 100 Years Ago." App.com. www.app.com.

———. "Jersey Shore Battered by Great Atlantic Hurricane of 1944." App.com. www.app.com.

Library of Congress. "Central R.R. of New Jersey—Sandy Hook route steamer, Sandy Hook, N.J." https://www.loc.gov.

Life-Saving Service Heritage Association. "Spermacetti Cove Life-Saving Station." www.uslife-savingservice.org.

Lighthouse Friends. "Sandy Hook Lighthouse." www.lighthousefriends.com.

Long Branch Free Public Library. www.longbranchlib.org/local-history.

Lumen Courses. "The Rise of Immigration." https://courses.lumenlearning.com.

Massey, James C., and Shirley Maxwell. "The Charm of Queen Anne Houses." Old House Online. www.oldhouseonline.com.

Middletown Township, New Jersey. "Monmouth Hills." www.middletownnj.org.

Middletown Township Public Library. *Red Bank Register*, February 8, 1888. http://rbr.mtpl.org/data/rbr/1880-1889/1888/1888.02.08.pdf.

———. *Red Bank Register* Newspaper Archives. Part 1, 1878–1923. Part 2, 1924–1991. http://rbr.mtpl.org/rbr.

Monmouth Beach Cultural Center. www.monmouthbeach.org.

Monmouth County Clerk. "Buildings in Monmouth: Stories and Styles." https://www.monmouthcountyclerk.com.

———. "New Jersey in Focus: The World War I Era, 1910–1920." www.monmouthcountyclerk.com.

Monmouth County Genealogy Society. http://sites.rootsweb.com/~njmcgs.

Monmouth County, New Jersey. "Middletown Survey and National Register Nomination Project." www.nj.gov.

Montreal Beach Resort. "Cape May, Settled by Whalers (& other cool facts)." www.montrealbeachresort.com.

PBS Learning Media. "First Encounters: The Lenape, Henry Hudson, and the Power of Objects." https://www.pbslearningmedia.org.

Potter, Derek. "Theme Park History: L.A. Thompson, the Father of the Themed Roller Coaster." Theme Park Insider. www.themeparkinsider.com.

The Press of Atlantic City. "First Electric Trolley Cars in New Jersey." www.pressofatlanticcity.com.

Princeton University Library. "Sanborn Maps of New Jersey: Highlands." www.library.princeton.edu.

Railroad.net. "Fort Hancock, Sandy Hook, NJ." www.railroad.net.

Sandy Hook Gateway National Recreation Area. "Highland Beach, New Jersey: A Jersey Shore Destination, 1881–1962." National Park Service. www.nps.gov.

———. "An Oral History Interview with Harry Sandlass, Sandlass Beach Club." www.nps.gov.

———. "An Oral History Interview with John Mulhern: 1908–1927." National Park Service. www.nps.org.

Santoro, Lisa. "The Upper-Class Brooklyn Resorts of the Victorian Era." Curbed.com. www.ny.curbed.com.

Shipping Law Blog. "What Is the Difference between a Boat, a Ship, and a Vessel?" July 3, 2010. www.theshippinglawblog.com.

———. "What Is the Difference Between an Oil Rig and an Oil Platform." www.theshippinglawblog.com.

Shirley, David. "Jersey Shore Is Awash with Architectural Gems." *New York Times*, August 2, 1981. www.nytimes.

Smith, Muriel J. "Atlantic Highlands' Tribute to Cooper's Water Witch." *Atlantic Highlands Herald*, May 8, 2017. www.ahherald.com.

This Old House. "Jersey Shore Rebuilds." www.thisoldhouse.com.

Troy, Gil. "The Surprisingly Glamorous History of New Jersey Presidential Vacations." Daily Beast. www.thedailybeast.com.

Toque Mag. "Rector's Restaurant, New York City." www.toquemag.com.

Township of Egg Harbor, New Jersey. "History." www.ehtgov.org.

Twin Lights Historic Site. www.visitnj.org.

Two River Times (Red Bank, NJ). "Monmouth County: The Jewish Newport of the Jersey Shore." https://tworivertimes.com.

USGenNet. "Points of History in Cape May County." http://www.usgennet.org.

Various newspapers. Highland Beach clippings, 1874–1905. Dropbox folders. www.dropbox.com/sh/foh8nju850782m0/AAA5XBvW78pVx7wvjxHDo7FMa?dl=0.

Various newspapers. Highland Beach clippings, 1906–1942. Dropbox folders. www.dropbox.com/sh/gm0pqmcyqalok79/AAChpEvBB7pLfeRIoLKgV8Ixa?dl=0.

Ward, John T. "Sandy Hook: Lost Resort Revived on Video." Redbank. www.redbankgreen.com.

Water Witch Club Historic District. Middletown Township, Monmouth County, Highlands, NJ 07732. www.livingplaces.com.

Wikipedia. "League of American Bicyclists." www.wikipedia.org.

———. "Monmouth Hills, New Jersey." www.en.wikipedia.org.

———. "Queen Anne style architecture." www.wikipedia.org.

———. "Sea Bright—Monmouth Beach Seawall." www.wikipedia.org.

INDEX

L

M

N

O

P

Q

R

S

T

V

W

ABOUT THE AUTHOR

Susan Gardiner is a co-founder of the Jersey Coast Heritage Museum, established in 2016. The nonprofit strives to create awareness of the history of the Highland Beach excursion resort as a vital legacy of the Jersey Shore. Susan actively supports the New Jersey Twin Lights Historical Society and its museum exhibits. She contributes artifacts and brings historical stories of interest to the public. Susan grew up in Sea Bright, New Jersey, and moved to Washington, D.C., in 1965.

For over twenty-five years, she was active in bilingual community outreach in the Montgomery County Public School System. As a community activist, she was awarded the Distinguished Service to Public Education by the Montgomery County Board of Education in 2014. She was recognized for her skills in providing community outreach to underserved families in the local schools. Her award-winning photography and her experience as a documentarian continue to enrich her pursuits. Susan is a mother of five children and a grandmother of ten. She lives with her husband, Gary, in Montgomery Village, Maryland.